Lessons from a Warzone

Lessons from a Warzone

How to Be a Resilient Leader in Times of Crisis

LOUAI AL ROUMANI

BUSINESS

PENGUIN BUSINESS

UK | USA | Canada | Ireland | Australia
India | New Zealand | South Africa

Penguin Business is part of the Penguin Random House group of companies
whose addresses can be found at global.penguinrandomhouse.com.

First published 2020
001

Typeset in 12/14.75 pt Dante MT Std
by Integra Software Services Pvt. Ltd, Pondicherry
Printed and bound in Great Britain by Clays Ltd, Elcograf S.p.A.

A CIP catalogue record for this book is available from the British Library

ISBN: 978-0-241-40485-0

Follow us on LinkedIn: linkedin.com/company/penguinbusiness

www.greenpenguin.co.uk

MIX
Paper from
responsible sources
FSC® C018179

Penguin Random House is committed to a
sustainable future for our business, our readers
and our planet. This book is made from Forest
Stewardship Council® certified paper.

To Mama, Baba, Nadeen, Zeina and Dana
الله يخليلي اياكن

Contents

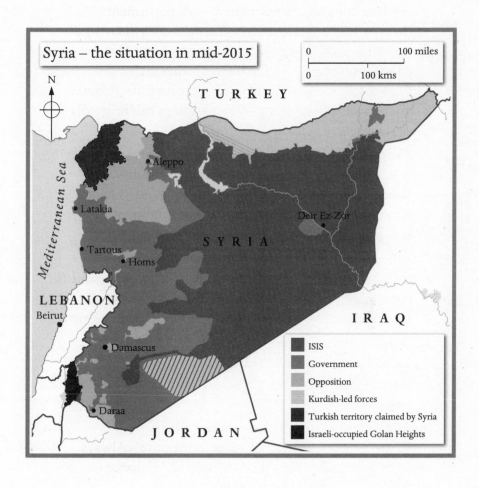

Syria – the situation in mid-2015

| | 0 | 100 miles |
| 0 | 100 kms | |

TURKEY

N

Aleppo

Mediterranean Sea

Latakia

Deir Ez-Zor

Tartous

SYRIA

Homs

LEBANON

Beirut

IRAQ

Damascus

Daraa

JORDAN

ISIS
Government
Opposition
Kurdish-led forces
Turkish territory claimed by Syria
Israeli-occupied Golan Heights

Preface: Pre-crisis

I had one request for my father in the summer of 1990 when we spoke on the phone one evening: to get me my He-Man toys from Kuwait. I was spending the last few weeks of the holidays with my sisters and mother in Damascus, Syria, as we did every year, before we had to return to Kuwait, where we lived. I was only nine, and my father was due to fly from Kuwait to visit us the next day.

Next morning, my grandfather woke me up and told me that my father wouldn't be able to make it that day. The Iraqi army had occupied Kuwait in the early hours of the morning and so Kuwait City airport was closed. I was too young back then to understand the political context, but I do recall some instances of sitting amongst my extended family in the preceding weeks as they discussed Saddam Hussein's threats to 'punish' Kuwait. I couldn't understand the references made to the earlier Iran–Iraq War and to the billions of dollars worth of dues that Saddam Hussein asked Kuwait to pay, as compensation for what he viewed as economic warfare undertaken by his much smaller neighbour. All that mattered to me, as a child, was to understand how everyone assuredly concluded that there was no way there was going to be a war: 'Akeed mafi harb – Definitely no war,' my grandfather would say to anyone who remotely questioned the possibility of war.

But war did happen. The ability to make international phone calls was soon severed in Kuwait, so we had no way to make contact with my father for almost a month, until the time he finally showed up, as a surprise, in our Damascus home. He had travelled by car through Iraq and Jordan, before eventually continuing his route to Syria. State relations between Iraq and Syria were at their lowest point ever, in light of the animosity between the different Baath parties that ruled Syria and Iraq. The Baath political party

xi

was a pan-Arab political party that ended up in power in both Iraq and Syria, but the different factions were far from being friends, as each viewed themselves as the solitary and 'true' representative of Baathist doctrines. The fact that Syria had also sided with Iran in the earlier Iraq–Iran War between 1980 and 1988 also exacerbated matters, and this trickled down to sour the relations between the two peoples at times. However, there was one thing about Syria that Iraqis never stopped liking: our soap operas.

My father, Ousama Al Roumani, was a renowned Syrian TV actor in the 1970s, and many of his soap operas, movies and plays had made their way to Iraq, which meant that during his journey through the warring country he was often jubilantly recognized at the otherwise-stringent Iraqi checkpoints. He had a pivotal role in one of Syria's most iconic theatre productions ever: *Gherbeh*, which was set in a fictional Arab village. In one of its quintessential scenes an annual one-day festival of 'lies' is celebrated, when both villagers and the government compete to tell the most blatant lie. My father's character, Abu Ahmad, sets off on a singing spree, sarcastically praising the government's feats and accomplishments in building schools, hospitals and providing jobs for everyone. The government representative then scolds him for uttering such an audacious lie, which even the deceitful government could not match. The scene's message resonated fervently across the Arab world, reaching even the most disgruntled Iraqi soldiers who had been sent to fight an unnecessary war. So when they encountered my father at the checkpoint, they would often forget the warfare for a minute or two as they asked him to recite a few memorable lines from that scene. He was always happy to oblige, not least because it greatly helped to facilitate his long journey home, where I rejoiced at finally seeing him. Some, but not all, of my He-Man action figures made it too, as my father had been forced to offer some of them as a token to soldiers on the route, who hoped to present them to their children. We would remain in Syria for two years, until Kuwait was liberated, returning only in the autumn of 1992.

People who have lived through the consequences of war typically have their life timelines polarized into two eras: one preceding the war and one during/after it. This polarization remained with me throughout my life, almost as though my memories had been divided between two boxes: one labelled 'pre-1990' and the other labelled 'post-1990'. The first thing I would think about, when recalling any distant memory, was whether it belonged in the former or the latter box.

Little did I know that another box would be opened twenty years later.

In the summer of 2010 I had just returned to Damascus from Boston, where I had completed my MBA, to re-join Banque Bemo Saudi Fransi (BBSF) – the bank that I had worked with for several years – as head of finance and planning. BBSF was the largest privately owned retail bank in Syria, and the first to open in the country. It was founded in 2004 by two regional banks – Banque Bemo from Lebanon, and Banque Saudi Fransi from Saudi Arabia – with a majority ownership of Syrian shareholders. Syria's banking sector had been completely dominated by state-owned banks ever since the 1960s, when the ruling governments adopted a socialist ideology, and so state nationalization took place and all privately owned banks were shut. Since the early 2000s, however, the country had started opening up, and private enterprise across all sectors was being encouraged.

Telecom companies, banks, malls, insurance companies and even an international fast-food chain began opening. People would queue outside KFC when it first opened in Damascus, and that reminded me of the long queues I had seen in Moscow as a tourist child, with my grandparents, outside McDonald's a few weeks before communist rule fell apart. It seemed a universal truth that people living under some form of planned economy where the government controlled most aspects of it were hungry for private enterprise. So when BBSF opened, people flocked to us with their money, and much eagerness, to deal with the budding private sector. Far from being a Wall Street-style global bank, similar to those that are sometimes demonized around the world, BBSF was a bank for Syrians from all walks of life, who entrusted us with their life savings. Unlike some other banks that opened after BBSF, we did not impose the need to maintain a minimum deposit balance. We did not want to be seen as 'selective'. Virtually any Syrian could open a bank account with us, so we had the richest Syrians and the poorest as our customers. From fishermen in the coastal city of Tartous, to shepherds near the Syrian desert-town of Deir ez-Zor and merchants in Damascus and Aleppo, everyone was calling BBSF 'the bank of the people'.

I had received a couple of intriguing job offers from a bank and from a leading consulting company in one of the Arab Gulf states, but I insisted on returning home from Boston. Though I had lived most of my life up to that point outside Syria, I was well attached to my country. And prospects in Syria were great back then. The economy was booming, foreign investments were flooding in and the country was poised for a Dubai-like renaissance. What was destined to be the largest mall in Syria, Lebanon and Jordan was being built in Yaafour, a lush Damascus suburb. A major Dubai-based construction company had purchased a large plot of land there and was building a vast complex of commercial buildings and towers, conjuring up visions of towering skylines similar to those in Dubai. Billboards all over Damascus boasted of the ambitious blueprints for the new stock-exchange building that was to open in that development. My sister worked as an exhibition-content developer back then, travelling to London to develop content for what was planned to be a one-of-a-kind children's science museum in the heart of Damascus – something that would have been completely new to the Middle East. The building was in the shape of a giant rose, reminiscent of the world-renowned damask rose, the beautiful (and edible) pink rose named after the city of Damascus, and which holds a special status in Syria. Such was the vibe in Syria at the time that I never thought twice about taking up an opportunity elsewhere.

Just a few months later we witnessed the unrest of the so-called 'Arab Spring', which erupted quite rapidly in neighbouring Egypt,

Tunisia and Libya. Early in 2011, the French CEO of BBSF asked a few of his trusted Syrian aides for an informal meeting. He wanted to know whether we thought such unrest would happen in Syria.

'Definitely not,' we all said. I was as reassuring as my grandfather had sounded, more than twenty years before, when he was asked whether a war would erupt between Iraq and Kuwait. We all agreed that unrest was unthinkable in Syria. Syria was 'different', we claimed. We fervently believed we were immune to those winds of change, and that such unrest would never occur. I was so certain of it that I took the decision to invest a large part of my savings in the Syrian stock exchange. Never did we imagine, as we sat in that air-conditioned boardroom sipping dark Turkish coffee, that not only would unrest break out in Syria just a few weeks later, but it would develop into one of the worst wars in modern times.

Syria was considered to be one of the safest countries in the region before the unrest in 2011. Today it is notorious for being the most dangerous country in the world. In March 2011, unrest erupted in the southern city of Daraa, where clashes took place between police forces and local residents. Unrest gradually spread across the country, before it escalated into a series of armed conflicts and later into full-blown war, with jihadists such as ISIS emerging in the power vacuums that occurred across the country. The complexity of the war triggered many fault lines within Syria in the most tragic ways possible, caused by sectarian, historical, economic and, of course, geopolitical factors.

The year of 2011 was to become my new 1990: a date that polarized my life again into two distinct chunks, pre-war and post-war. But this time I was no longer a nine-year-old child sheltered abroad from the consequences of the war, who could be reassured by my parents that 'everything is going to be okay'. I was on the ground, feeling the increasingly intense heat of the war as it gradually affected me across all parts of my life, transforming my perspective on everything.

When José Mourinho, one of the world's most prominent football coaches, was asked in 2013 about the disappointing results that his football team, Chelsea, showed back then, he said that Syria represented a crisis; his team losing a few games didn't. When a leading motivational and entrepreneurship speaker, known for his excessive cursing, was told that the situation of a particular business start-up was f***ed up, his response was that Syria was f***ed up; this situation wasn't.

Syria has become the metaphor for utter crisis, and even the world's greatest concede that it is an almost unfixable mess. When people are in trouble, they have the advantage of understating the challenges faced, by comparing it to a far more disheartening context: Syria.

Unfortunately for me, being part of the team that led the largest bank in Syria throughout the war meant that I had no other 'Syria' to serve as a benchmark for the most difficult of circumstances. This was probably as bad as it could get, and I had no choice but to adapt. I found myself in charge of planning at the bank, in the most conflict-ridden country in the world. I still had some of the Harvard business cases and articles that I had discussed in class the previous year during my MBA, and I hurriedly dug them out and started going through them, looking hopelessly for solutions.

I could not find solutions – in the articles on 'agile organizations' and 'rules for change management' – for the type of strategic and operational challenges that we were facing. I met up with my university professor, whom I had revered highly in Beirut, where I studied for my Bachelor's degree some ten years back, but was dismayed when the first piece of advice he gave me was the textbook response 'change your company by-laws', which was irrelevant and did not address the operational and strategic difficulties we were facing.

I bought a few crisis-management books, but realized that most of them dealt either with the consequences of the financial crisis or with unique crisis situations resulting from product recalls or PR failures. While the financial crisis has proven dire and demanding for many companies to adapt to, and especially for banks, the challenges we faced – operating in an actual war – seemed far more colossal.

In war, almost everything is thrown into question. It is tremendously difficult to make any assumptions, because anything can change at any moment. The unthinkable becomes thinkable. Things become a thousand times tougher. While in the past we might have had plans to deal with a currency depreciation of 5 per cent, in the current situation we could face a radical 500 per cent depreciation. Business 'threats' were no longer attributed to reduced commercial opportunities, but to increased mortar-bomb attacks from terrorists such as ISIS, who for a long time were situated just a twenty-minute ride away from my office in central Damascus. Whereas previously we would engage in re-forecasting exercises and questioning assumptions when dealing with 'normal' uncertain variables or business threats, as many businesses in the world do, this crisis was fundamentally and structurally different from any other crisis addressed in any business literature.

It was under these increasingly tough circumstances that I led, intermittently, the finance, strategy and operations functions of BBSF, from the outbreak of the war in 2011 until the early summer of 2015. At the outset we had a staff count of around 700 employees and thirty-nine branches across the country. The bank operated (and continues to do so) under a highly regulated environment, with corporate governance laws similar to those in place in many developed economies, manifested in the creation of board committees and segregation of the roles of chairman and CEO. My last position was as the bank's Chief Financial Officer (CFO) entrusted with leading the strategic planning of the bank in addition to the oversight of the finance function. I was part of the executive management that collectively took decisions on all high-level matters headed by the CEO, who in turn reported to bank's board of directors.

When I meet people in London, where I now live with my wife Nadeen, many seem surprised when they find out that banks were actually operating during the war – and still are in Syria. They are even more surprised when I tell them that not only are banks operating, but a couple of them are actually doing very well. And some people are shocked to learn that the bank I worked for not only managed to safeguard the life savings of its customer base, but also flourished strategically during the war, so much that it became almost impossible for other banks to catch up.

With time, and in this exceptional context, I found myself learning unique lessons about how to become more resilient in the face of adversity – some of those lessons clashing with textbook rules, whereas others drifted along varying trajectories. I therefore decided to write this book to share the lessons I had learned from working in such tough times. It is not meant to be a technical treatise on crisis-management methods, or a guidebook for managing a bank or a corporation in dire times or in war-ridden countries. And it is definitely not meant to be a celebration of my own 'heroics' – those insights that I have developed have been influenced not only by my own actions, but also by those taken by my brave colleagues at all levels.

Try searching for BBSF in English on YouTube and you will come across a series of corporate-style motivational videos developed by the bank's human resources department. Do the same search in Arabic and the results will be terrifying. The first video in the list shows fearsome jihadist soldiers clad in black in the eastern city of Deir ez-Zor, walking through the rubble of one of our demolished branches with their black banners, with one of the leading men screaming the bank's name through his two-way radio as he informs his commander of their latest conquest: the bank. Luckily we had air-lifted the safe-deposit boxes of that branch a few days earlier, in an operation that no insurance policy in the world would cover. When we told our customers with safe-deposit boxes to collect their items from our Damascus branch, they could not believe that their valuables had been saved. We were rewarded with what the Bedouin Arabs from that area have been renowned for, over the past 1,500 years: poems. Tens of poems praising the bank's vigour filled our corporate walls. No one in the world generally likes banks, let alone in a crisis. However, Syrians from all walks of life loved us, and we had the framed poems to prove it.

The difficulties we faced were not part of a cyclical slump in the market. This wasn't a temporary chaos stemming from a PR failure or a product recall, or a scandal linked to a top executive. It was beyond crisis management. Syria was probably the worst place ever in the world to do business in, let alone to flourish and prosper.

This book is part-memoir, part-business book, which shares ten strategic business lessons learned in an almost-unmatched experience within an exceptionally demanding context. Sometimes the lessons I learned seem counter-intuitive – such as not using the word 'survival' in the worst of times, and trying hard to shock our systems on purpose. There were also unlikely sources of inspiration, one of which arose from observing the changing patterns of the Syrian military checkpoints.

It is my hope that this book will help you learn profound lessons in business strategy and resilience. I hope it will show how, even when things seem at their worst, good things or even better things can happen, with the right mindset.

Businesses are dynamic, and every business is bound to go through turbulence or tough times at some point. The challenges facing organizations around the world are different, but I believe that many of the principles concerning how to face a crisis are universal. You might ask how a learning experience in Syria, with so many uniquely peculiar challenges, can apply to you, working in a start-up in New York or London. My response is that the heightened state of intensity and frequency of disruptions that I faced, in one of the most difficult environments, made the learning far more profound than it would probably be in an otherwise less chaotic context. The lessons we learn in life usually happen at critical times. The more critical the context, the more valuable the learning experience may become. War triggers shocks to both the internal and external systems of an organization, in so many directions, in a way that hardly ever occurs in other circumstances. This increases your exposure to many different scenarios and accelerates the learning process, adding clarity concerning what really matters and what doesn't. This is what happens when ISIS are just twenty minutes away.

The pace of the learning curve in a crisis is usually slow, as it rarely lasts for a persistently long time or becomes the default state of operations. In my experience, working in an extremely adverse situation for a long time expedited the pace of my learning curve. You do not have to go through a war, or even be facing tough times, to find at least some of these lessons relevant; but knowing them might prove useful in the event of turbulent or tough times ahead, no matter where in the world you are or what your business does.

I also have another motivation for writing this book. Syria has become a news story for the wrong reasons. Most of the voices originating from it are legitimate voices of sorrow, agony and pain, and Syria is largely portrayed in the media as a place devoid of hope.

I want to offer a different voice – hopefully one of insight and intrigue – as I highlight an experience that is rarely relayed at such times. While there are 'lessons to be learned' from the conflict in Syria, concerning social, humanitarian, political and other domains, hardly anyone addresses the lessons learned in leadership, crisis management and resilience. The context is unique, in its challenges to leadership and organizational resilience, and is something that is rarely addressed. I try my best not to make any political statements in this book. There are thousands of Syria-related political analysts; the world does not need another one. Such statements also lie outside the scope of this book.

A popular Syrian proverb says, 'It is better to learn from a doer than from an expert.' I humbly consider myself the former. If you wish to read about strategies for managing in times of crisis and adversity, written by academics or other writers whose fieldwork consists of research undertaken in the libraries of grand universities in London, Oxford and Boston, then this book might not be for you.

This is not the work of a foreign journalist who spent a few days at the Four Seasons Hotel in Damascus, chatting with some taxi drivers, and ended up writing about the 'pulse of the people'. This is the 'pulse itself' – originally written in the English language – where I talk about the pragmatic and experience-driven lessons learned on the ground, from one of the most hostile environments in the world: the war-battered streets of Syria.

I see it as a story of hope, perseverance and the relentless pursuit of triumph in the direst circumstances. At BBSF we fell, we made mistakes and we had our flaws. But we did not stop there. Not only did the bank remain resilient throughout a period when other banks faltered, but it thrived. A strategic rift emerged, in such a way that it became almost impossible for other banks to catch up – a feat that was almost unthinkable in peaceful times, let alone during such a war. We transcended the conventional competitive-positioning dynamics; we became warrior poets, worthy of the most emotional of Bedouin poems. This is the story of how we did it.

خيم الليل والذيب بان نابه / قلنا ضاع الحلال و المال و نعيمه
قصدنا رب السما يسخر لنا حبابه / جانا الفرج من نشامى بنك بيمو

As the dark night dawned on us, the wolf's fangs emerged
We conceded the loss of our money, blessings and belongings
We prayed to God for a loving helping hand
And we were saved by the chivalrous heroes of Banque Bemo.

One of the poems we received from a customer after we returned his rescued valuables, stored in our safe-deposit boxes in Deir ez-Zor

Don't do things right; do the right thing

Many turning points, but no turning back

I often get asked about the 'turning point' of my time in war-ridden Syria. People expect that one dramatic story led to a complete shift, or even to an upheaval of my perspectives and circumstances. The truth of the matter is that the crisis steadily unfolded, layer by layer, revealing new complications and posing fresh difficulties across many areas. The transformation was not a dramatic leap between an absolute world of order and one of complete mayhem.

Looking back, I recall the accumulation of many small moments that represented a series of turning points, each changing a part of me in one way or another. Most of them represented 'first time' incidents for me – you tend to recall the first time you have experienced almost anything that has happened to you. I remember the time I saw the initial signs of unrest on television – it unsettled my view of Syria's stability. Then came the long queues at banks across the country – these altered my view on the robustness of a sector that was growing, and had seemed indestructible a few weeks earlier. Then the first manned military checkpoint – I had seen Syrian military checkpoints in Lebanon in the 1990s, but for some reason I never expected to see them in Syria. And the first time my family thought I had been kidnapped – I had exceeded the limit on my Internet data, so my SIM card was deactivated for an hour, during which my parents tried in vain to call me and assumed the worst had happened. The first time I heard a mortar bomb – now I know how to differentiate between an incoming and an outgoing bomb. The first time I saw a mortar bomb – you don't really see it, you just feel its aftermath. The first time I almost got hit by a mortar bomb – I froze for ten minutes and couldn't say a word. I also remember the second time – I froze for less time, five minutes, and I was able to say a word or two.

There were many 'first times', and each one brought with it a transformation in perspective, a learning outcome and an improvement in my coping mechanism. Each was profound in its own way, shaping the manner in which I viewed everything around me.

One very profound moment came in the summer of 2012, just over a year after the unrest had first started. The war now felt closer and more intimate in Damascus. A big bombing occurred in an upscale neighbourhood of the city and ripped apart the headquarters where a meeting of senior military members was taking place. Four of the most senior commanders, including the defence minister, died. This was the first major sign that the war had entered the heart of Damascus and clearly signified that it was not coming to an end any time soon. It had actually only just started.

At that stage both my parents and those of my fiancée left Damascus. My mother and sisters initially moved to Beirut, before joining my father in Kuwait. My soon-to-be in-laws left for Riyadh. In war, typically the elder ones stay and the younger ones flee to start new lives abroad. I had it the other way round. There was something that felt unnatural about living in my own city without my parents. My home town was always synonymous with my family. It was I who used to leave the city, never my parents. I left to study in Beirut and later in Boston. I was a variable, but my home town and family were a constant and were always linked together, so Damascus suddenly felt eerily different. The high point of the absurdity of this feeling came when I spent the first night of my life in a hotel in my own home town.

Kidnappings became more common that summer in Damascus, and living on my own meant that I was safest in a central hotel a stone's throw from the bank. I remember very well my first day at the hotel. I consider it my first day of being a Syrian immigrant, a refugee of some sort who could no longer live in safety in his own home in his home town. Check-ins are typically the least memorable moments of a hotel stay, but I could not forget this check-in, as it signified the beginning of a new relationship between me and my home town. How could I spend a night at a hotel in my own city? Hotels are for when you travel; they are in far-away places that you are either there to explore for fun or to undertake some business in. You should never have to spend a night in a hotel in the place where you live permanently, especially when your home is just a few kilometres away.

I couldn't sleep that night. I lit a cigarette by the hotel-room's window and looked at the imposing Mount Qasioun with its rugged hills, which has overlooked Damascus for thousands of years. The founding of Rome has the legend of the brothers Romulus and Remus. Less well known is the mystical legend concerning the founding of Damascus by the biblical brothers Qain and Abel. There are many stories behind the founding of the city, and my favourite is this one. Legend has it the Garden of Eden was here. Qain, the son of Adam, struck his brother Abel near this very mountain of Qasioun. As Abel's blood struck the earth, the first murder in the world was committed. The earth had not seen murder-blood before and, with the first few spills of Abel's blood, the stones split apart in anguish, thus giving birth to the Semitic name of Damascus: *Dam-shak*. Even today in Arabic *dam* means 'blood' and *shak* means 'tore apart'. There is even a burial shrine for Abel near the mountain.

When I used to gaze at the back of the mountain from my own bedroom window, before the war, I would summon up the mythical images of the lush Garden of Eden that speak the story of Damascus. From my hotel-room window, however, the view was similar, but the recollection became strikingly different. As I looked upon the same mountain, the glorious image of gardens dispersed, to be replaced by a more fitting image. I could no longer imagine the lush gardens; all I could see was the image of two brothers killing each other over this land.

This was the new Syria that I had to become accustomed to.

To bank or not to bank?

'Know thyself' – two simple words by Socrates that have survived timelessly through the years. Self-awareness is key, whether you work in orderly times or in turbulent ones. Knowing yourself, to determine whether or not it is strategically worth navigating a crisis, is fundamental. Not everyone should plunge themselves into navigating a crisis.

All privately owned banks in Syria were founded by large regional banking groups. At the outset of the war, BBSF was the largest privately owned bank in Syria, whereas our founding banks were not the biggest banks in their respective countries. In terms of balance-sheet size, our founders were much larger than us, but we outgrew our founders, in the sense that we became much more prominent in our country of operation than they ever did in their own.

When the first unrest started in the southern city of Daraa, people flocked to withdraw their deposits from banks across the country, and many borrowers stopped paying back their loans. Across the region, systematic political upheavals had taken place in Egypt, Libya and Tunisia. The prospects of a looming and troublesome crisis unfolded and a strategic decision had to be made by banks.

Some banks had a small presence in Syria, which constituted a not-so-significant addition to their regional network. For them, managing Syria was too big a headache and was not worth it. They probably had a large risk appetite for other matters, but Syria did not matter much to them in the bigger picture; they simply did not have the risk willingness. A strategic decision to clamp down on operations and become incredibly risk-averse was taken. They decided not to bank – and that worked for them. Banks that took half-hearted approaches in reacting to the crisis eventually ended up in the worst of conditions, as we will see later in this book.

For us, it was different. BBSF was the only bank that was born out of two founding banks. It seemed an unlikely marriage of sorts:

a medium-sized private bank in Lebanon joined hands with a much larger commercial Saudi Arabian bank, with significant French ownership, and decided to create a bank that opened its doors in Syria in the early days of 2004.

This unique make-up actually made BBSF more independent than those banks that were established by one founding bank, as we were not just another subsidiary of a regional bank. We had developed a distinct identity that was different from that of both founders; we did not have our values and culture transposed from either of them. BBSF's culture was born organically from the day we started operating in Syria in 2004. It was a natural and, most importantly, authentic process that reflected all facets of our journey. Technically the founding banks jointly controlled BBSF, but our unique composition meant that on the ground we felt we enjoyed some sovereignty, which our founders actually cherished and came to see as representing a core advantage that needed to be built upon, rather than 'fixed'. We had something belonging to 'us' at the Syrian bank that we had to fight for. We had to soar through this crisis; it was almost as if we had no other choice. I don't remember witnessing a discussion about whether or not it was an option.

Assuming you determine that it is strategically worth navigating this crisis, it becomes tempting to say that you need to draw a line from the start, concerning what to do and when to do it. I know I did that myself, as I used to say, 'I will leave Syria the moment I hear a mortar bomb.' I ended up staying in Syria for four years after I heard my first mortar bomb.

I learned that there is a major complication to this approach. You are dynamic. You change. A crisis is likely to stretch you and transform you, and will become a valuable learning experience. Why let your pre-crisis self place limitations on your future self? Why should the growth of your future self be inhibited by your current perspective? Don't set limits on yourself. Don't draw red lines that end up shackling you. The types of challenges we face evolve in so many different ways, and along such different trajectories, that drawing a line before embarking on a crisis will confine you to the perceived limits as you think you know them now. The means by which you achieve your goals will sometimes be novel and challenging, and you will find yourself evolving with evolving times.

Looking back now, from the comfort of my London home to which I moved in 2015, I embrace the challenges that I have gone through. Make no mistake: no one enjoys working in a crisis. But crisis, or any form of turbulent time, is sometimes part of the cycle of any business. Operating in a crisis can become a very enriching and rewarding experience. With this mindset, you allow yourself to be driven to a relentless pursuit of triumph. It makes you almost ruthlessly aware, with much clarity about what really matters and what doesn't; and it makes you choose to do the right thing, as opposed to 'doing things right' – just as some banks did, when faced with a counterfeit-banknote dilemma.

The counterfeit-banknote dilemma

One could understand much of Syria's rich history through its intricately designed banknotes, which feature representations of ancient Byzantine mosaics, Crusader castles bulging towards the Mediterranean, and Assyrian cuneiform tablets. The tablets were preserved thanks essentially to a crisis that erupted in Syria and Iraq around 3,000 years ago. At the demise of the Assyrian Empire its imperial libraries were set ablaze, destroying much of what was there, except for the clay cuneiform tablets, which baked amidst the fires and thus lasted for thousands of years. Had they been written on some form of paper that was available at the time, they would have perished. While the fire burned everything else, it imparted the tablets with the resilience to make them last through time. Part of me would like to think that the Assyrians used clay on purpose to preserve their work and literature in the event of a crisis, but this is a far-fetched assumption. Sometimes sheer luck can be the main source of resilience. Mostly, however, as I came to learn, it is not.

Fast-forward a few thousand years, and Syrian banknotes are far less resilient than Assyrian cuneiform tablets. Behind all their elaborate design, one thing really mattered: whether or not these banknotes were genuine. The production of counterfeit banknotes grew from the outset of the war, posing significant challenges to banks. European sanctions were imposed on all Syrian government entities, including civilian ones, such as the Central Bank of Syria. In brief, this meant that European entities were generally not allowed to contract with Syrian governmental entities. So the Central Bank of Syria could not print banknotes in Western Europe any more, as it used to, and so they were printed elsewhere, with diminished quality. The banking regulators, being as stringent as they were, issued a law that instructed banks to call the police every time a client submitted a counterfeit banknote. Depositing the equivalent of a $1 banknote that you might have received unknowingly, as change from a baker, could therefore land you in a Syrian jail.

Banks sometimes received such counterfeit banknotes from some of their renowned clients, but knew that many of these clients were unaware that their banknotes were fake. This was especially true when just a couple of counterfeit banknotes out of a whole stack were fake. What were the banks to do? The instructions were clear: calling the police would have been 'doing things right'. But the banks knew they were not operating in normal times, when it was expected that the client in hand would be subjected to an undeniably fair and just trial. With increasing corruption and disorder in applying the law, the way this matter was going to be handled was most likely going to be harshly severe.

Most banks decided to do the right thing by simply bringing this matter to the attention of the client. They advised clients to be more vigilant in future, so that they never carried such counterfeits, and told them what signs to look out for to identify them. Technically it was doing something against the applicable law;

ethically, however, it made sense, and in the context it undeniably felt like the right thing to do.

To manage the bank during the war, we learned to become more disposed to take such decisions. In normal times, social, ethical and legal dynamics tend to be more or less aligned, posing few difficult dilemmas. In times of crisis, however, there are bound to be overlaps between these dynamics, in such a way that makes it less straight-forward to know what to do. We learned that our capacity to use our judgement and let it override other concerns was essential, even if it meant that this went against certain 'best practices', rules or regulations. We had to resist the fixation on doing things 'by the book', and had to rewire our mindsets so that the cliché was redefined to mean doing the right thing always. We came to learn that doing the right thing does not entail engaging in harmful action or behaviour; rather, in the example given above – of clients submitting counter-feit banknotes – a potentially harmful outcome would have happened, had the banks acted as legally required. We learned that by changing along those lines we were navigating our way in this evolving crisis, which continuously presented shifty dilemmas.

I learned that doing the right thing also propels you to be more noble – like the time we decided to offer our competitors' staff a bus ride.

Why we offered our competitors' staff a bus ride

Nobuaki Notohara is a Japanese author who has lived for many years in different countries in the Arab world and recollects in his book *The Arabs from a Japanese Perspective* his observations on Arabs. I believe it is the only book written originally in Arabic by a Japan-ese writer.

One of the things that seems to completely astound Notohara is the generosity and hospitality of Arabs; it is something he has never seen before. In Syria, in its heyday, it was normal for a bus driver to allow tourists on the bus without asking them to pay for the ride.

Tourists were sometimes baffled when they were offered free tea, or invited home for a big lunch by a family they had just met. While many cultures are renowned for being friendly, this seemingly 'excessive' generosity and hospitality towards the foreign guest are probably unique to many Arab cultures.

People remember and cherish generosity and noble behaviour – remember how good it felt the last time you received a free dessert at a restaurant, or got a free cup of coffee from your favourite barista. There is a certain gratification that arises when you are on the receiving end of generous acts.

Arab generosity is engrained deep in their culture and has a valid explanation. The early Arabs, living in their uninviting deserts, were mostly nomadic in nature. They roamed their scorched surroundings with limited access to water and food. They would sometimes spend several days without finding an oasis to obtain water from, while occasionally crossing paths with other roaming tribes. This harsh way of life led to the development of a particular code of honour, whereby roaming tribes would offer their guests, or whomever they met on the way, water and food. It created a give-and-take mentality – one time you were on the giving end, and on a different day you were bound to be on the receiving end. There was an expectation of reciprocity and this sustained the code of honour until it became a deep-rooted characteristic, exhibited even today by urban Arabs.

In times of crisis, resources become more finite, orderliness declines and people become more and more driven by self-interest. Noble and magnanimous behaviour becomes rarer, as fewer people can afford its luxury. At the same time, though, it becomes even more cherished when you exhibit it in difficult times. This trait is dominant across almost all cultures. We sometimes overstate the cost of nobility. It need not be extravagant. All it takes is a genuine effort to instil magnanimous behaviour in all that you do.

A couple of years into the war, transportation in Damascus became more and more difficult. Many public buses went out of service and fuel was in very short supply. Military checkpoints were clogging up the major streets. People were queuing in their cars at petrol stations for hours, hoping for a litre or two of over-priced fuel. Taxi prices soared dramatically. Taking a taxi also became a riskier endeavour, in the light of increasing kidnapping. It became not unusual for an employee of our bank to spend around one-third or more of his or her salary on transportation, in addition to two to three difficult hours each day on the road. We decided to rent a few buses on selected routes to ensure the pick-up and drop-off of BBSF's staff. This was something that was really appreciated.

We then decided to take things up a notch, in defiance of what 'best practice' prescribes. When we had empty space on the bus, we would take with us the employees of neighbouring competitor banks who did not have their own employee buses. This behaviour embarrassed and baffled the management of these competitor banks. Here we were, offering a much-needed service to their own employees for free! As this service meant a lot to staff, word quickly spread. Such a small behaviour greatly magnified our reputation as a good employer. At the same time our actions created confusion among our competitors, which ultimately led some of them to come up with their own transportation for their staff, as it was too excru-ciating to have us continue transporting their staff. Even when they started their own buses and their staff stopped using ours, we were still viewed as the initiators, as it was thanks to us that the staff were able to come to work in a much more convenient way. Our actions led to a positive contagious effect, which transcended the conven-tional competitive dynamics. We were looked up to, and many of our competitor banks' staff wanted to work for us.

This display of nobility in hard times was much appreciated, and it really did not cost us much. It also did not cripple our competi-tiveness. Being magnanimous does not imply being lenient in your competitiveness. Recall the iconic scene in the film *Lawrence of Arabia* when T. E. Lawrence and his Arab guide were drinking from the well of Sherif Ali (played by Omar Sharif). As Sherif Ali comes galloping in on his horse in the background, he reaches for his gun and shoots dead the Arab guide. Lawrence is flabbergasted. 'Why?' he asks. Sherif Ali tells him it's because the guide stole from his well. When Lawrence tells him that he drank from it too, the response he gets is: 'You are welcome.' This scene has become one of the most iconic in movie history. Far from perpetuating a problematic stereotype and endorsing this particular kind of behaviour by Sherif Ali, I mention it as it shows symbolically how Bedouins can be extremely hospitable when they welcome guests, but ruthless when others try to steal what belongs to them. Having the ability to know when to be ruthless and when you can afford some magnanimity becomes key.

Business is an ever-changing environment: one day you might be powerful, and on another day the chips may totally tilt to the other side; just as the harsh deserts imposed a reciprocal code of honour on its Bedouin inhabitants, so a crisis can impose a similar harsh context. One day, when you find yourself in need of support, any past noble acts will lure others to come and help you out. You will need to build bridges and forge friendships with everyone in such times. In war the structural landscape of society as a whole changed so drastically that I found unexpected people in unexpected places. 'Warlords' are not the only people to 'suddenly' emerge in war; lords come in different forms and shapes. I found new business traders, new manufacturers, new restaurateurs and even new barbers emerge, seemingly out of nowhere. But they do not in fact emerge out of nowhere. They emerge out of a complex network facilitated by changing variables in a crisis. Before the war I used to ignore my car mechanic's phone calls, as he always attempted to sell me an upgrade of my tyres. During the war, he turned into a successful household power-generator merchant, selling these much-needed devices at a time when blackouts became common, and suddenly he had the stronger bargaining power and stopped answering my frequent calls. I learned the hard way (and in darkness several times) that ensuring that you have good relationships with everyone becomes even more important in times of crisis.

When working in difficult times – but hopefully nowhere as extreme as the ones we faced in Syria – you will be offered opportunities to demonstrate noble behaviour. If you do not see them, then seek them out. Nobility is always memorable for the receiving end, and people will remember for ever the positivity that came from you in their darkest days; therefore leaving an honourable mark whenever you can is almost always the right thing to do. Nobility does not make you look weak and need not be a costly endeavour. Across all cultures, nobility is almost always well revered and respected. So exhibit it as much as you can. When in difficult times people can visibly see you being noble, they are likely to associate you with being simply better.

In other times, however, you will need to do things that will infuriate people, but they will probably thank you later. You will need to shock your systems on purpose – including, for example, hacking your own IT department. This definitely does not come under 'doing things right'.

Why it sometimes pays to hack your own IT department

I was in charge of stress-testing the bank's liquidity, which before the war entailed building statistical models where I would imagine several cash-related scenarios and incorporate different elements, to see how the bank's liquidity would evolve in these different scenarios.

The fact of the matter was that this exercise was very enjoyable and was not 'stressful', as the name implies. With my team, I would develop statistical models showcasing outcomes that would reassure everyone that stress-testing was done and the results were satisfactory.

Although my stress tests were statistically satisfying when reported as information, they had no impact on enhancing the bank's ability to withstand stress and shocks. Drawing models and fancy graphs does not improve resilience by itself. This is not to say that the recommendations derived from these models do not lead to decisions about enhancing certain aspects of the business; sometimes they do, but I learned in a context of adversity that an additional approach would be required.

In such times the challenges are very different from the challenges in normal times; you need to enhance the organization's overall ability to withstand the shocks that you are destined to face. Building models in a controlled environment will not improve this ability. One good way to do this is to continually and intentionally shock the system.

The turning point for me came when I realized how meaningless my 'beautiful' models were, when the war started and our liquidity began to deteriorate significantly. All my assumed variables and extrapolated figures proved quite useless. Forecasting future trends based on historical precedents assumes an extrapolation of the past context into the future. In a crisis this was not applicable, as the underlying dynamics of the past had no resemblance to the context of the future, which rendered all extrapolations misleading. If you are engaging in similar stress-testing or planning models at a time of crisis, which extrapolate the future based on past figures in 'normal times' that have now become irrelevant, you might need to stop doing that, even if it seems as if you're doing things right.

To build resilience and become more and more robust, you need to be subjected to actual shocks. That is the 'right' thing to do. You cannot build muscles by watching numerous videos of how-to-build-muscles exercise; it could lead you to observe and better learn the techniques, but no effect on your body takes place unless you actually start to exercise and lift weights yourself. Your muscles grow only when you subject them to gradually increasing stress. Your body's immunity develops over time only when you have subjected it to numerous bacterial infections. Roman emperors used to take gradually increasing doses of venom to improve their tolerance to poison, in case someone slipped venom in one of their drinks one day. This practice was later coined

'Mithridatism', after Mithridates VI, the King of Pontus, which was a part of the Roman Empire.

The best way to effectively improve your ability to withstand shocks is by being subjected to shocks yourself, and not solely by learning about them in controlled environments.

If you ask your IT department about your system's vulnerability to hacking, you will probably receive sufficient assurance that things are okay the way they are. If you ask them to stress-test this system, you will probably receive a well-written report with clear-cut diagrams showing how their firewalls have successfully intercepted hypothetically imagined hacks, with the exception of a couple of minor ones that will be addressed shortly. I am not questioning the credibility of the IT staff; it is just that I have seen in many instances how corporate employees are propelled to be inherently reassuring and to project scenarios that fall within their comfortable realms. Try pinching yourself; you will almost always stop at the very moment when it starts to become painful. If I were to ask you if pinching is painful or unpleasant, assuming that you have never been pinched by someone else, then the sensation you get from pinching yourself would not be representative of the sensation felt when someone else pinches you, as they would probably pinch you much harder.

So, back to the IT department. To really stress-test it, agree with a third party on a 'friendly' hack, without your IT people knowing about it. Your IT department might initially panic; it's okay, though. Only good will come from it, for a successful hack will reveal weaknesses and enable your IT department to fix them and improve on themselves. It will make your people more robust, now that they have had a taste of what it feels to get a shock for real that does not correspond with the scenarios they have projected. If the hack does not go through, then you know your system is on par and that any deficiencies can be fixed. Your staff will become more alert and prepared for the real thing, if it ever happens. It may sound a little cruel, but in a crisis such shocks improve your ability to manage unexpected surprises and build organic resilience in a way that tests in a controlled environment can hardly do. They make you so much better prepared, in case the real thing ever happens.

In another example, let's assume you run a retail store of some sort and your branch staff have attended a coaching course on innovative thinking – and thinking outside the box – facilitated by a bubbly life-coach. The life-coach was highly inspirational, and many students came up with innovative solutions to imagined scenarios, after they had drawn them on the flipboards that life-coaches seem to love so much and had explained them to their peers. Very good. Your staff have also just undertaken training in how to implement certain procedures, in case of a major power cut. In this example, you operate in a crisis where power blackouts are a real threat.

Now it's time to test your staff's ability to think outside the box and apply the new procedures. This needs to be done in real-time, and not in a comfortable hotel meeting room or corporate conference room in a controlled environment. Choose a time when your branch is not busy with clients and when disruption is not critical to your operations, then cut the power supply on purpose, without your staff knowing about it. This might sound cruel and even brutal, but remember that if you are working in adverse situations, and if this scenario is likely to take place at some point, then you need to ensure that your staff know how to react properly.

Your staff will feel uncomfortable. Will they be able to apply on the spot the procedures they have learned in a controlled environment? Will they be able to continue to serve their clients? Or will they decide to stop everything and tell your clients that they are unable to serve them now? Your staff will be subjected to a real-life stress that is powerful enough to weigh their capacity to make decisions, but not overwhelming enough to hamper your operational affairs. It will be interesting for you to see how they react. If you do this more than once, you will probably be surprised at how quickly your staff become more and more accustomed to shocks, the more they are subjected to them; and how increasingly creative they become at adapting to them.

Of course you shouldn't be shocking all your systems haphazardly just for the fun of it. Identify the systems and areas of operations that are vulnerable and likely to be affected by the crisis, and where reliance on their continuity is essential to your operations. Subjecting them to occasional shocks will make your staff more comfortable at dealing with uncertainty and whatever it entails, and this skill needs to be nourished to prepare them for real-life surprising, stressful situations that could occur. The discipline of operational resilience today generally focuses on controlled exercises, and I understand why they are used in stable environments and how they are probably better than doing nothing. However, I have learned that actual shocks are the best creators of resilient people and systems. I understand that different cultures and schools of thought might view this differently, and I respect that. These situations have made me more robust and resilient than any *Harvard Business Review* article on resilience that I have read. For me, it is doing the right thing.

Doing the right thing also entails playing the long game, which requires a transformation of your concept of time to allow your long-term goals to preside over more immediate short-term goals. This takes us to our second chapter. But first here are some questions to ask yourself at the outset of an unfolding crisis:

- Strategically, and looking at the big picture, is this crisis worth navigating? Do you have the option of exiting, if it is *not* worth navigating?
- Are you inclined to self-impose limits from the start on what to do and what not to do? Do you think these might limit your future self?
- What opportunities can you seek out to exhibit noble behaviour? What does it cost you to be noble? Do you think people will cherish nobility more, or less, in times of crisis? How do you think you will be remembered if you leave an honourable mark in difficult times?

- What is the downside to intentionally shocking some of the systems in place that have become more vulnerable in the crisis? What is the upside? Can the upside be achieved instead in controlled environments?

2

Transform your concept of time

Old State House in Boston versus my grandfather's house in Damascus

The Old State House in downtown Boston was just a stone's throw away from where I lived in 2009 while I was studying for my MBA. As I walked every day to the nearby underground station to go to my classes, I would see queues of people walking along the Freedom Trail (a four-kilometre path in downtown Boston that passes sixteen historical locations) and snapping photos of the modest-looking building. Intrigued by it, I looked up the building's history. It turns out that it was constructed in the early eighteenth century and is the oldest-surviving public building in Boston; it is also one of the oldest buildings in the US. In the eyes of Americans and much of the 'New World', this rare building of 300 years of age is seen as ancient.

This differed greatly from my own perspective. Hailing from what most scholars agree is the oldest continually inhabited city in the world, I have always been deeply aware that Damascus is thousands of years old, and this formed an essential part of my identity and social consciousness. Some structures in the city date back hundreds of years, if not a couple of thousand. There is nothing extraordinary about a building that is 300 years old; my grandfather's parents' house is probably older.

Most of the cultures of the 'New World', with their much shorter history and less distant cultural and civilizational developments, tend to adopt a more short-term outlook on life, with a yearning for immediate consequences. In many 'Old World' cultures, however, the knowledge of their long history involuntarily embeds within people an appreciation of their place in time. It shapes their perspective towards the future, knowing that the accumulated cultural and civilizational acumen they possess is one that was built slowly over thousands of years. The business term 'Confucian dynamism' was developed in reference to the teachings of the ancient Chinese thinker Confucius (551–479 BC). It refers to a spectrum in which different cultures are categorized depending on the extent by which their long-term focus presides over their short-term outlook. This focus on the short term becomes more noticeable when one views how management best practices in the West perceive the concept of time.

Time goes beyond fiscal years

In the corporate world, management is inclined to view time as being chunks of fiscal years. The short term is generally viewed as representing a year at most, whereas the distant long term usually refers to a period of five years at most. But even while associated with a period of just five years, any long-term ideas that are presented – whether they represent prospects, opportunities or risks – are usually discussed in an abstract form by businesses, as if they are a lifetime away.

The reality is that five years is really a very short time. Think about the last time a small project was implemented in your organization, whether it was a change of software or the revamp of a process. It probably took a couple of years, from inception to completion and training of all those involved. Operational changes can take a few years to materialize fully, and yet many modern business practices entail planning for the next fiscal year, with a terminal date where all targets and metrics need to materialize consummately, as if time comes to an end right afterwards. Most of those businesses that do plan a little further ahead usually do so in the form of a midterm plan that spans an extended period of three years, in which certain indicators are proposed that will measure the well-being of the company. Accountants and even financial managers are programmed to view the future in terms of increments of fiscal years, and many are fixated on the achievement of budgeted targets in the current year, over everything else.

When managing BBSF during the Syrian war we learned that this notion of time needs to be transformed – and radically so. Time is not an extension of chunks of fiscal years, with December of every year (or April in the UK, as I found out, to my surprise) needing to become a major strategic milestone. With war raging epically a few kilometres away from us in the suburbs of Damascus, we learned to recognize that eventually it would end. All wars end; some take a hundred years, like the legendary one between France and England in the fourteenth and fifteenth centuries, while others end after a few months. We approached our business knowing that, in spite of the gruelling circumstances, difficult times would eventually come to an end.

Rather than advocating *against* planning for the short term, or *for* planning budgets for the next twenty years, the overriding framework should not stem from year-end goals and targets, but from a long-term vision and strategic objectives. Defining these becomes the most pressing and challenging task. Its difficulty lies not in being able to determine the timeframe and outcome of the war in our case, or in any other crisis, as it is unlikely you will be able to do so with much precision. And in any case, this is not what is important. The difficulty lies in being able to identify the strategic core elements that you believe will make your business sustainable, regardless of the different situations.

Knowing the Critical Success Factors (CSFs) of your industry – and how their criticality shifts in a crisis – is of the utmost importance.

Why we stopped asking when the war would end

At the outset of the war we were asking in meeting rooms:

- When will the war end?
- How will it end?
- Will the US interfere?

All these questions had hundreds of possible answers – none of them conclusive. It was easy to get swept away spending hours discussing the certainty of these hypothetical scenarios. We later learned that they were futile attempts at formulating our business strategy.

With time, we learned to ask more effective fundamental questions, such as:

- What are the Critical Success Factors (CSFs) in this industry, assuming there was no war today?

At BBSF we had to have an understanding of the Critical Success Factors of the banking industry. CSFs refer to the set of features that a company should get right in order to become competitive. In Syria's banking sector, for example, having a high-liquidity ratio and a low cost of funds represented Critical Success Factors. Simply put, this meant having enough cash reserves from deposits at a cheap price.

- If the war ends tomorrow, or in ten years, would these CSFs still be critical?

The answer here was 'Yes'.

War is epically destructive – and yet it is a phase. A temporary phase. If we viewed the atrocious Syrian war as a phase, then there is probably no excuse for anyone in the world not to view their own crisis similarly. War is destructive, but it does not necessarily destroy an industry's general dynamics. It is likely to lead to a shift in the criticality of some factors and to difficulty in fulfilling them. There will be particular factors pertaining to each country or industry that could have distinct effects on these CSFs and they should be considered, but they would in many cases concern operational and tactical challenges rather than high-level strategic ones.

In the bank we had previously determined that having the lowest cost of funds would always be a Critical Success Factor that would set us apart from the competition, regardless of the outcome of the war. A bank lends money. People still need to borrow, and would like to do so at the cheapest rate possible. Having the lowest cost of funds, or money at a cheap price, would put us in a favourable position to be able to lend to clients at a far more competitive rate than other banks. This holds true before war, during war and after war. Whether the war ends tomorrow or in ten or one hundred years, there will probably be no change in the validity of this statement. Whether the US, Russia or Papua New Guinea interferes, this industry dynamic is unlikely to change.

Having high liquidity, or in other words high cash reserves, was also identified as an integral CSF. You can only lend when you have enough funds. This is true today, tomorrow and probably for ever. What changed was that before the war almost all banks had comfortable liquidity levels, so all banks fulfilled this critical requirement quite easily. A bank could not really differentiate itself having this advantage. This success factor was therefore always critical, but less so as a means of differentiation before the war. When the war started and bank run-ons took place – when people flocked to withdraw their deposits, as we will see later in the book – this success factor shifted to become much more comparatively critical than before.

Thus consideration of the timeline of the war becomes less relevant when effort should instead be exerted towards identifying the CSFs and determining their shifting criticality. Asking when the war would end became almost a pointless exercise, because there was no way we could find out, no matter how many political analysts we asked.

Another Critical Success Factor that we determined was trust. Banking is built on trust; this was true for the first commercial banks in sixteenth-century Renaissance Venice and it is true today. No person in their right mind would trust you with their life's savings if they did not trust that you will protect them. Regardless of when the war ends, we asked whether trust and public perception are important. The answer again was a simple 'Yes'. In spite of the radical changes that have taken place in Syria's demographics – from internal and external displacement to the tragically high number of deaths and injuries – we determined that the public perception of those in Syria with banking needs during the war always values trust significantly. Yes, perhaps a significant part of the pre-war population has stopped having banking needs, due to circumstances beyond their control. However, for those who remain in need of banking, and those who will have banking needs in the future, trust increasingly became an even more Critical Success Factor. As such, we decided that in whatever we did and no matter what the context was, gaining and maintaining the trust of the public was a CSF.

It's not always about the money

- Is being profitable a Critical Success Factor today?

After much deliberation, we arrived at the conclusion that it is not. There will be pressure for immediate returns, even more so in war-time, due to increasing demands from many shareholders in increasingly difficult times. However, we found it essential to rewire our mindset to transform the notion of time, and believe in the necessity of compromising on our profitability to sustain excelling at our CSFs. Ultimately, your aim is to maximize the long-term wealth of shareholders, and in adverse times this will probably entail sacrificing short-term gain to help you achieve this goal. This is very difficult to agree on, because many shareholders are typically keen on maximizing returns as soon as possible and find that annual profit-linked targets are the best indicators for assessing the performance of managers. They are also, rightly, aware that if improving profitability stops being a goal, then it becomes easier for managers to slack. This is why key shareholders and managers should engage in this strategic discussion early on, to manage expectations and agree on which metrics will be deemed import-ant and which ones will be used to assess performance. More on this, and on alignment, in the last chapter of the book (see page 141).

Appreciation of the long-term aspect of your business becomes of paramount importance here. We learned to resist the temptation to get stuck solely on fulfilling short-term targets. Business will become more and more difficult, and even constructing a budget for the next three months will prove an elusive job, let alone pre-paring a forecast for a longer period. However, all you must do should stem from a Confucius-like understanding of the future. It was difficult to train ourselves not to ask the ever-tempting, useless questions that no one in the world has the correct answer to. In the film *Bridge of Spies*, Tom Hanks, who plays the role of a lawyer defending a Soviet spy in the US, asks the spy, just before the court is due to give its sentence, if he is worried. 'Would it help?' the spy asks. Similarly, we trained ourselves to stop asking questions that we had no answers to, or ones that added no value.

Play the long game like a third-generation family business does

We saw how other competing banks reacted. Some became so obsessed at fulfilling short-term targets that they took action to momentarily improve their profitability, at the expense of killing their capabilities and diminishing their competitiveness with regard to the CSFs. Some banks stopped paying good rates on their deposits, to save on their interest expense; it temporarily led to cost savings, but eroded their deposits, as their clients pulled them away, rendering the banks unable to lend competitively. The banks ended up saving money for a few months, offering temporary causes for celebration for the managers who were able to improve their profit-ability targets, before discovering a few months later that they had crippled their bank's competitiveness and found it much harder to keep up in the long run.

Many businesses, in many different business contexts around the world, tend to exhibit this short-termism. What the war did was to accelerate the behavioural pace of the different banks, with the consequences being much more immediately and rapidly manifested than they would have been in other contexts. And so it became much clearer to us how focusing on short-term targets, rather than having your action stemming from a long-term strategic objective, could destroy a company's capability.

We do not fully realize that the biggest corporations in the world today are relatively young institutions, compared to much more deep-rooted institutions around the world, such as universities and governments. Concepts of management practice are also relatively young and are nowhere near as developed as social, political and philosophical disciplines that have evolved over hundreds and even thousands of years. As such, many corporations are still unaccustomed to thinking that far ahead, as they still have not accumulated a long historical legacy. Planning for generations in advance, as clichéd as it sounds, should be what corporations and companies engage in, regardless of the context. Family businesses that are run by third and fourth generations recognize the importance of adapting a long-term vision because they see their success as a continuation of what their forefathers did tens of years ago, and they assess the success of their own actions by the impact they imagine these will have on their grandchildren, tens of years on from now. What is intriguing is that across different world cultures this particular outlook seems to be dominant amongst third- and fourth-generation family businesses. I have met such people across the world – ranging from English families who have never bought furniture, because this is always inherited, to Syrian families who have been doing the same trade since Ottoman times, more than a hundred years ago. When one of them decides to buy a watch, for example, their decision is based on how they imagine this watch will look on their grandchild's hand many years later. They tend to approach their businesses similarly. They may do things that might not yield a return for the next couple of years or so, but which will help to build a legacy that will propel the growth of their business twenty years later.

This deviates greatly from the behaviour of many salaried managers, whose actions are governed by short-term motivations that are mostly linked to profit metrics. To them, what happens beyond that terminal year-end date on which certain metrics determine their bonuses may become almost irrelevant. This is why alignment is key, and this will be addressed in Chapter 10.

In adverse times, we learned that adopting this sense of appreciation of time and long-term focus becomes more and more important, because the daily challenges could easily have tempted us to lose touch with the future.

Even in normal times, you should wire yourself to enable your long-term aspirations to shape your actions, and not the other way around. Liberate yourself from viewing your corporate success in the future being embodied by hitting a sales target by year-end; this detail will be trivial in the long-term life of your organization. Many corporations today might very well continue to be present for the next hundreds of years. Therefore foregoing a profitability target in a certain year to ensure the fulfilment of more strategic goals should rein you in and take the upper hand. For every strategic decision you take, consider its long-term effect. It seems like a very simple thing to say, yet it is scarcely done in business. Measuring the short-term cost saving or incremental revenue increase of any decision is usually much easier and, as such, generally takes precedence. We are inclined to take the easy route, because very few of us are comfortable with ambiguity. Assessing the long-term impact of how this decision affects your long-term value, and asking the right questions, is much harder to do; but is much more essential.

We learned that embedding this Confucian concept of time within our culture and within the decision-making process is vital, otherwise we would have been swept away into taking easy short-term decisions in order to 'survive', while unknowingly our actions would be diminishing the value of our own company in the longer run.

Keeping an eye out for the long term does not mean, however, that you lose touch with what is going on today; on the contrary, in times of crisis you need to have an even sharper eye to identify business opportunities. This leads us to the third chapter, but first here are some questions to ask yourself as you reflect on the concept of time and find yourself querying the timeline of a crisis:

- Do you think this crisis will eventually be over?
- Are you asking questions about the timeline of the crisis? Does anyone know the answer? How helpful is it to ask questions on the crisis or the context, over which you have no control?
- What are the Critical Success Factors of your industry? How has their criticality changed? How valid are they now? How valid will they be, assuming the crisis persists for another year? How about if it lasts for another five years? Based on that, should your actions fulfil them?
- Do you let your actions today shape your long-term aspirations or the other way round? Which do you think is better?
- What do you think a third-generation family business does differently from other conventional businesses? Do you think it assesses the success of its actions based on their short-term impact or a much longer-term impact?
- If your goal is to maximize shareholder wealth in the long run, are there areas where you could be better off sacrificing short-term profitability, if that builds long-term value?

3

Chase opportunities relentlessly and don't die until death comes to you

The souq must go on

On a rainy day in late 2013 my wife Nadeen called me and asked me to get from the old souq in Damascus some jasmine home scent fragrance to spray around our home. Going shopping in the souq on rainy days is always a clumsy affair; the rustic metal roofs are filled with holes, said to have been caused by bullets from French and Ottoman soldiers, although it makes more sense to me for them to have been punctured on purpose at some point, to enable sunlight to pass through. Whatever caused them, their inconvenience that day was that they let in the rain. Carrying an umbrella in a tight souq, where people brush shoulders as they walk by, is not a good idea; I had to prepare to get soaked.

I hurried off to the souq after work, walked past the Street-called-Straight, one of the oldest continuously functional streets in the world, which was even mentioned in the Bible, and headed to the perfume seller. The young seller was talking to a woman who was negotiating hard for some perfumes. I stood patiently behind, observing the different scents available while allowing my thoughts to drift off. A few kilometres away in the suburbs raging battles were being held, yet here you could easily spend an hour choosing from among a hundred different flower-essence perfumes. An almost eerie sense of normalcy dawned on me, before it slowly left, after I noticed an old man sitting behind the young seller; I guessed he was the seller's father. The man was seemingly in his eighties, resting in a very dignified manner on a wooden stool and holding an old cane with his left hand. He sat there silently, yet piercingly, observing the interaction between his son and the woman buyer. He looked timeless to me. I could imagine that same person sitting in that same spot ten years ago, a hundred years ago, and even more than two thousand years ago when the street received its biblical mention, observing his son trying to sell a woman a perfume. Suddenly the context seemed less relevant. The souq must go on, whatever happened.

The two largest cities in Syria are Aleppo and Damascus, and long before they had been made famous by the war, their rivalry revolved around which was the oldest continuously inhabited city in the world. Not the oldest per se, because excavations have revealed older settlements, but the oldest to be *continuously* inhabited. This uninterrupted flow of human settlement and interaction in one of the most eventful regions in the world has to mean something. In spite of all the crumbling empires and raging wars, their strong mercantile nature enabled these cities to live on and sustain their growth through time. It seems that you can destroy a city in this part of the world a thousand times and the first thing to re-emerge is its souq. Little surprise then that this is one of the few Arabic words that is recognizable in almost any other language.

As I mused on this, the woman continued her bickering negotiation. The seller politely refused to give her a discount. She ultimately bought her items and walked away. It was now my turn. I knew exactly what I wanted. I told the seller what I needed. He told me about a new scent they had been making: I smelled it out of curiosity and then politely refused. I bought quite a lot of perfume, to last us as long as possible – I wasn't in the mood for returning here any time soon. When I enquired about the total price, I was asked to pay 3,000 Syrian pounds. Usually I would haggle – it seems almost instinctive in the souq. But this time I didn't. Business was bad and there had been virtually no tourists for the past two years or so. The local currency was diminishing in value. I also had a very good job, when others weren't so lucky. So it just didn't seem right. I immediately gave the seller 3,000

Syrian pounds. As I took the bags and started to leave, the old man spoke for the first time, commanding his son, 'Give him back two hundred pounds. Don't offer a discount to those who haggle. Give it to those who don't.'

This was pure souq wisdom. Souq sellers don't need MBAs or need to hear about client-centric processes. Serving their clients the right way is something embedded in their DNA for hundreds of years.

When clients rushed to withdraw their money from banks at the outset of the crisis, at BBSF we did the exact opposite of what distressed banks in Greece, Cyprus and Argentina did. It was as if our souq heritage was dictating to us what to do.

Why we embraced our clients' panic to withdraw their money

A bank run-on refers to when clients rush to withdraw money from a bank. It usually happens in times of uncertainty or distress, when people start fearing for the safety of their savings, triggered either by a systematic shake to the entire banking sector or by a specific bank fumbling. It is a bank's nightmare, as banks keep in cash only a very small portion of their deposits, calculated by complicated algorithms and governed by strict laws. The rest of their funds are invested to make profit, mostly in the form of lending, but also in other financial instruments. The complication of a run-on is that besides putting pressure on the bank's liquidity, it puts most pressure on the bank's reputation and thus triggers a frightening vicious cycle. If the bank is unable to meet the need to give depositors their cash, then it risks gaining the worst reputation ever: 'This bank doesn't have any money.' If it doesn't have any money, then people are much less likely to trust the bank with their savings. A decreasing base of depositors means a decreasing base of borrowers, and so the entire operations of that bank will shrink. Operational complications can be resolved, whereas reputational ones are much harder.

Another thing about run-ons is that they happen very early on in a crisis – they are almost the perfect barometer for any looming catastrophe. All it took was the first two weeks of unrest in small parts of Syria for a systematic run-on to unleash itself across the country. This was well before the conflict developed into a fully fledged war, and even before the currency started depreciating in value. Almost every business owner loves to see a queue of customers lining up outside their store or branch, especially if they start lining up a couple of hours before opening. Not so a bank. Long queues outside a bank spell trouble.

As has happened elsewhere in distressed times, some banks in Syria started to impose limits on daily withdrawals, or put policies in place to delay withdrawals. If you came in to withdraw a total of one million Syrian pounds, you would be told to withdraw one hundred thousand pounds each day over ten days. In one way or another the banks were trying to outsmart their clients, to force them into keeping their money with them for as long as possible.

We took a different approach. Many of these clients had their life savings with us. People were scared and panicking. Nothing could really comfort them. Would we impose limits on withdrawals? Would we delay client withdrawals? Would we try and convince our clients not to panic and give them a false sense of assurance that there was no crisis? Who were we, anyway, to belittle the crisis around us? Who were we to know something about the overall crisis that our clients didn't? It would have displayed a conceited and almost deceitful sense of arrogance and, worst of all, an unbearably groundless know-it-all attitude, which people in a crisis get repelled by the most. So we decided not to.

To counter the ever-growing queues of people lining up to withdraw their money, we decided to stack our banknotes next to the glass counters, so that they were visible to everyone in our branches. We wanted everyone to see our money – and that we had plenty of it. For any client who wanted to withdraw one million Syrian pounds (around US $20,000 back then), we made sure they had it straight away. No delays and no pushy persuasion techniques to convince clients to keep their money with us.

In a crisis, your clients are likely to react fast. Many will take decisions that you may find irrational. In our case, they were in a state of shock. You have to keep in mind that however unfounded these decisions may seem to you, they have been perfectly rationalized in your clients' heads. They are panicking and they are acting protectively. The worst thing you can do is to refute their distress and try to outsmart them, especially in our case, when the matter concerned something so fundamentally important as their savings. For many of the banks that tried to do that, the result was that their clients overwhelmingly persisted until they withdrew what they wanted to, or even more than they initially set out to withdraw. Those who wanted to withdraw half of what they owned actually ended up withdrawing all their money, following those attempts to convince them otherwise.

Our approach, however, comforted our clients; our money was out there and visible to all. We accommodated the panic of our clients and did not attempt to contest it foolishly; we understood their motives and knew we couldn't really convince them otherwise. They were scared and we let them exercise their fear, while making sure that we told them they were welcome to bring their money back whenever they felt comfortable to do so. We made sure it looked as if it was a 'given' that we would always be there, willing to take back their deposits whenever they felt it was safe to do so. We did not take action to show that we had a funding crisis, although in practice we did stretch ourselves to make sure we had enough funds across all our branches to meet the growing demand. Tempting as it was, we would not allow increasing operational challenges to dictate our course of action, as that would mean that we were not putting our clients at the forefront. Moreover, we let everyone see our large stacks of money – there was nothing to hide. We had plenty of cash for everyone, and we wanted them to see that and talk about it.

Most banks saw their liquidity ratios drop below the legally required ratio – that is the amount of cash they needed to have in relation to their deposits. We didn't. A few months in, our liquidity ratio actually started to slightly improve. Clients who had withdrawn money from us started bringing it back. Clients from other banks that had tried to outsmart them had heard about our stacks of banknotes, and our approach in letting people withdraw their money, and came to us. We did not try to outsmart our clients; we let them act the way they wanted to. This is how genuine trust is instilled. People know when you try to outsmart them or push them into an action that will make them feel uncomfortable. In normal times, they might politely resist you. In a crisis they might come to hate you. At the outset of our policy, we were criticized by some for not being client-centric and not engaging in client retention, as we let many of our customers leave with their money. Our response was simple: our action represented the pinnacle of client retention; we addressed and responded to their fervent need for cash. We learned that by making our cash more visible, sometimes exaggeratedly so, we signalled an aura of confidence to our customers. In difficult times, if you attempt to downplay your clients' genuine fear and panic and try to outsmart them, they will come to hate you and will stray away.

Sharpening our capacity to put customers at the forefront of everything was fundamental to us. After that, it became imperative to search for viable opportunities around us, despite the gruelling context.

First-timers

Nations have different personalities, built slowly over the years, and this forms an essential part of their identity, whether or not they are consciously aware of it. Syria is thousands of years old, yet it never had a strong sense of governance. Except for some short-lived episodes in time, no Syrian ever really ruled Syria – as we know it today – until the mid-twentieth century; we were always absorbed within some larger empire, whether it was the ancient Egyptian, Greek, Persian or Roman Empire, until the twentieth century, when Syria became independent. Even when Damascus ruled a large part of the world through the Umayyad Empire in Islam's golden age in the seventh and eighth centuries AD, it was a newly arriving Arab dynasty from the Arabian peninsula that founded this empire. Why the people of this region had no strong autonomous governance is the topic for another book. At the same time, this region gave birth to many innovations in the world.

Farming is widely accepted to have started in the rivers between Syria and Iraq. We created the first alphabet. We allegedly created the first musical note. This historical trait of pursuing opportunities enabled us to be the first to invent many things, and to become incredibly versatile and adaptive, with little regard to the overriding politics. This became, almost unknowingly, part of our psyche. Finding opportunities anywhere, in spite of the difficulties, is probably one of the most Syrian attributes ever – perhaps that is how our main cities sustained themselves through all the times when other cities fell, and so became the oldest *continuously* inhabited cities in the world. This probably also explains why at BBSF we offered housing loans when Syrians were leaving the country.

Why we offered housing loans when Syrians were escaping the country

When you operate in adverse times, ideas or images that highlight the negatives will become more and more pervasive and entrenched in people's minds. In normal situations we are subject to this logical fallacy whereby we are sometimes inclined to block certain information and unnecessarily eclipse the significance of one fact over another. In a crisis, that effect is likely to become magnified. The devastating images of wholly destroyed cities in Syria, with refugees in long lines pushing across European borders, have taken deep root in people's minds, that you might be tempted to conclude that this represents the entire Syrian scene. Sadly, those scenes of destruction are true; many people perished and lost their homes. The suffering was real. The scenes were so harsh that it became easy to have your perspective polarized. In times of crisis, this is what you need to work on and resist falling into. It becomes all too easy to get carried away with the overall scene and dismiss the specifics. It becomes much harder to analyse the situation impartially, with all its dynamics.

At the height of the crisis we did something that many people found unusual, and some even comical. We launched a housing loan to enable Syrian immigrants to buy a house in Syria. There had always been Syrians living overseas before the crisis, mostly working in the Gulf, and many with lucrative jobs and incomes. Houses in Syria were always seen to be expensive. With the unrest, prices went down. The local currency also depreciated, meaning that someone who was earning their income outside Syria would be able to purchase more Syrian pounds with the same amount of foreign currency. In our advertisement for housing loans, we put the emphasis on paying in the local currency: 'Your home in your homeland' was the main motto, with an image of a house drawn on a Syrian pound coin. At a glance it appealed to people's patriotism in emotionally fervent times; but more importantly, the message was that your house would be paid for in Syrian pounds, which were cheap then. It was a bargain for those who were based outside Syria. It also meant that we were lending money to those who were unaffected by the war, so we were able to identify a potential group of customers who were far less risky than the ones we were currently dealing with.

Yes, there was a lot of destruction in Syria. There are varying statistics, and one of the more popular ones states that almost one-third of all houses in the country have been destroyed and around half of its people displaced. One out of every two Syrians had to forcibly leave their home, and one out of every three houses was destroyed – these are tormenting figures that the world has not seen elsewhere in contemporary times. In such an environment it takes little for businesses to stop searching for opportunities.

At BBSF we started to view things differently. One out of every three houses was destroyed: that meant the remaining two were still there. One out of every two Syrians had to move home, so we asked: what about the Syrians who were outside Syria? Did they have a favourable advantage now? A statistic presented in such a way might skew your way of looking at things; so saying that one out of three houses was destroyed might lead you to imagine a street where one-third of the houses are destroyed and the others are standing. Further scrutiny reveals a different pattern, however. Destruction was mainly concentrated in certain areas, and many parts of the country were not subjected to such destruction, and still, houses there became much cheaper. There were cheap real-estate prices, a 'cheap' currency, and established Syrians abroad whose work was not affected by the unrest in Syria. As such, we identified a market and launched a product to play into these factors. It was not aimed at the fleeing Syrians. There have always been a significant number of Syrians living abroad, even before the unrest, and we only needed to be able to lend to a few. We were able to identify an opportunity, create a market for it and service it effectively. Besides the actual business gained in launching such a housing loan, the signalling effect it triggered was perhaps even more important. It was a sign of persistence, because not only did we not cut our activities, but we searched overseas as we relentlessly chased opportunities.

Don't die until death comes to you

As I will repeatedly mention in this book, it is imperative that you do not get swept away by the general mood, because in times of crisis the mood is bound to become low and circumstances are likely to evoke misery more than inspiration. There is no doubt that it is easier to be innovative in inspirational settings, but since you are not working in such settings, you will have to exert extra effort. Encouraging the generation of ideas – no matter how ludicrous they might sound at first – is essential. Fostering such an environment amongst your team is crucial. Such ideas must be analysed to the very specifics, and you must not allow the overriding tide of general disbelief to wash them away. There will always be opportunities in every environment, even amidst one like Syria's horrific war.

Power cuts became so plentiful in Syria that many houses would get electricity for only a couple of hours a day. A mediocre banker would literally see the dark side of this; more capable bankers, however, saw the opportunity to finance the newly emerging and very profitable industry of residential power generators.

Such difficult times should stimulate you to become more innovative and refine your capability to identify new trends, develop novel products and service new markets. Being bold is essential. A Syrian proverb says, 'Don't die until death comes to you.' I have seen so many instances where companies in Syria, out of wanting to 'survive', plunge themselves prematurely into death. This includes the banks that have decided to 'halt all lending activities' because of the prevailing increased risk. A bank is supposed to lend money. Increasing risk should be countered with increasing risk management, not with ceasing the provision of your core offering altogether. The actions that many of these companies undertook, while initially justified as acts of survival, turned out in reality to be more like suicidal acts.

Market challenges and the risks faced will become harder to combat, meaning that you should step up your game and not let go, the moment it becomes harder to operate. The rigour required will only intensify as times become more and more difficult, and so refining your capability to identify opportunities and act with boldness can set you far apart from the competition.

When you are identifying opportunities in such circumstances, it becomes important to focus on what creates the most impact. A crisis disrupts many things, including the 80/20 rule.

The 80/20 rule becomes a 95/5 rule in a crisis

People I meet in London are often surprised as to how banks continue to operate in Syria as we speak, and even more so when they learn that a couple are actually doing really well. Almost instinctively, people recall the scenes of destruction they have seen on television, and the large groups of escaping refugees, and this leads many to conclude that there can't possibly be an environment where banks can continue to operate. I don't really blame them, as I would have probably thought the same, if I were in their shoes.

There is no denying that large parts of Syria have seen utter destruction. Unfortunately several cities and towns have seen so much demolition that it would be difficult to imagine them being built again. Yet in spite of all this destruction and even the exodus of people, there are still millions of people living in Syria today. These people have to wake up, commute to work (for the lucky ones who still have work), eat and engage in whatever daily activities they do. So the war has definitely taken its toll significantly on the economy, but there are still economic cycles in play to ensure that people can commute, eat and try to live as normal a life as the situation enables them to do. In spite of sanctions and logistic difficulties, food still needs to be produced, imported, transported and consumed. Even the warring parties in Syria sometimes trade with each other; in spite of their ideological differences, they pretty much agree on where the best food ingredients come from. So rebel-held areas need the sun-drenched tomatoes from Syria's government-controlled southern region, just as much as government-held areas need the pistachios and olive oil grown in Syria's rebel strongholds. They fight ferociously, but they also allow some trade to occur between themselves. People across the country still need to drink coffee, tea and maté (the Argentinian drink that, uncannily, found its way to many homes by means of Syrian immigrants) every day. Consumption and investment as a whole have reduced, but they nevertheless continue to exist in many areas. These cycles need to be financed, and there are viable opportunities for banking. The successful banks leveraged on this diminishing but viable window of opportunity wherever possible; the unsuccessful ones went with the flow of the overall narrative and inhibited their actions and were therefore unable to find these small windows of opportunity.

Bankers joke that the difficulty in banking lies in the fact that they engage in basically two tasks, one of which is the easiest thing in the world to do, and the other the most difficult thing in the world. The former is lending people money: hold out a US $100 bill and stand on any pavement on any street in the world and offer to lend it. You will not be disappointed. However, getting back this $100 will prove to be a far more difficult endeavour – just ask anyone who's ever lent money. In the bank's case in Syria, the effect of both actions was amplified. More people would jump at the opportunity to borrow money, and more of these people would be less able, or even less willing, to pay it back. Add to that the reduced ability in many instances to enforce laws and regulations in the bank's favour, or to trigger punitive measures, such as selling mortgaged land, if this land suddenly came under the control of ISIS. Increasingly, working in adverse times will prove difficult. So choosing your clients becomes even more important.

Let's say there are twenty-three million people in Syria (there are no reliable statistics since the war started, so this is a rough hypothetical estimate) – a bank can still take in deposits from hundreds of thousands of people. As for lending, it does not need to lend to all these hundreds of thousands in order to be very successful. In normal times the Pareto rule states that roughly 80 per cent of effects stem from 20 per cent of the causes. So transferring this principle to clients, 20 per cent of your clients would give you 80 per cent of your revenue.

In adverse times, and with the radical change in the environment, I observed at first hand how this rule seems to change from

80/20 to 95/5: 5 per cent of clients would generate 95 per cent of revenue. This increases the concentration risk, but when viewed from a positive angle, enhances your ability to better manage your most important clients and makes you more focused.

In difficult times, the effect of polarization becomes more and more manifest across most areas. In Syria I saw how the poorer became poorer and the rich became richer. Some areas were destroyed, whereas others became even more beautiful. Distribution of power, income and standards of living became ever more polarized. And this transcended to business.

Ultimately, the exact evolution of this rule might not work out to be precisely that drastic. What matters is that fewer constituents will lead to more effects, and you have to be prepared to be more focused and revamp your ability to narrow down, and continuously identify the decreasing, yet more powerful base of clients. Their number is less, but their capacity to generate value to you has compounded. As such, you have to act fast, and far more competitively. Service these clients and ensure that you retain them and increase their business. Successful clients in difficult times have proven that they are resilient and are more likely to sustain their good performance. Being part of their success is of paramount importance to you. Be flexible in your pricing, ensure they are more than satisfied, and even consider making short-term small losses for the benefit of long-term strategic partnership.

In addition to retaining your best customers, you need to ensure that you have the right information systems that will enable you to break down accurately the profitability per channel, platform and customer. You need to identify this winning 5 per cent niche, and this is far more difficult than doing so for the top 20 per cent, but can prove to be far more rewarding. Your information system must be on par with this new reality, and able to present accurately and in good time to you the effects of this top 5 per cent stratum. You need to be able to identify the top 5 per cent of your clients, your staff, your channels, your products and your cost drivers.

Wire your brain to think and analyse using this newly emerging 95/5 rule to identify viable opportunities and your work will be more focused on what matters most. And maybe, just maybe, this could be the best time to create a strategic rift in a way that would have been unimaginable in normal times. This takes us on to the fourth chapter, but first here are some questions to ask yourself as you deliberate on the merits of chasing opportunities in tough times:

- If your clients become more reactive or distressed, do you try to outsmart them? In a crisis are you inclined to do more of that? What happens if instead you accommodate their concerns? What actions can you take to instil trust in what you do, even if your clients momentarily steer away?
- Do you let your operational challenges dictate your actions? Or do your objectives dictate the means by which you manage your operational challenges?
- In a crisis do you allow the negatives to dominate the overall landscape? Are you still able to identify opportunities, even if they have become less visible?
- Do you foster an environment that encourages the generation of ideas and the pursuit of opportunities? As the mood is low, do you allow the overall tides of disbelief around you to wash away any small but viable windows of opportunity? How does this affect your competitiveness?
- How do you face higher risks? With increasing risk management? Or by limiting your core offering? How does limiting your core offering affect your competitiveness?
- How is the crisis affecting the 80/20 rule? Does it still apply? Or is it becoming more skewed? Is your analysis

shifting, with the shift in this rule? If it is turning into a 95/5 rule, are you able to identify the top 5 per cent of your clients, your staff, your channels, your products and your cost drivers?

4

Now could be the best time to create a strategic rift

No one likes a crisis

Let me clarify one thing at this stage. I do not look forward to working in a crisis. My message will never be along the lines of those 'motivational' speakers and writers who make statements like 'Crisis is opportunity in disguise.' A crisis is far from being an enjoyable experience. The belittling and whitewashing of a crisis can be insulting to those who have been through the pain and agony of a very difficult one. It is not an opportunity in disguise.

In life some things happen, whether we like them or not. I lived very happily in Syria before the war and never had any thought of ever living elsewhere. I had a great job that I loved, I was near family and friends, and although I travelled a lot, I always enjoyed returning home.

However, I was unlucky enough to be part of the Syrian generation that had to experience one of the worst contemporary wars. I could not stop the war; the crisis befell us. At the bank, we had to act and adapt accordingly, but I can safely say that no one I worked with ever looked forward to it. We managed to find opportunities in the crisis, despite the difficulties it presented. We understood, with time and a lot of mistakes on the way, that there are certain principles to follow that will greatly improve your chances of flourishing in a crisis and that will make the best use of any available opportunities. One of the things we learned is that despite the difficulties we encountered, now could be the best time to create a strategic rift. Yes – during a crisis. When a crisis looms and is unavoidable, like a strong wave approaching you in the middle of the sea, how you respond decides the outcome. The wave can overwhelm you, or if you learn to ride along with it, it can enable you to soar to heights you wouldn't otherwise have reached.

Soar amidst the disruption

In some instances you could find yourself in a much more strategically favourable position in a crisis than in regular times.

A situation happened in our bank where we found ourselves offering an increasingly demanded service, without consciously knowingly so at first. Due to the worsening of the security situation, physical transportation across cities became more and more difficult. So the transport of people and goods became much harder throughout the country. The transportation of banknotes became a far riskier and more difficult endeavour. As BBSF had the largest network of bank branches in Syria, we noticed that some of our clients started transferring money to our different branches much more frequently than before. A client in our Aleppo branch might deposit a certain sum that could be withdrawn by any other client of their choice in Damascus one hour later. Effectively our existing infrastructure, branch network and banking services empowered us with a Critical Success Factor pertaining to the industry of cash transfers, without us voluntarily doing anything about it. Since we had the biggest network of branches among privately owned banks, we found ourselves naturally able to differentiate ourselves with this service. The crisis had unexpectedly positioned us in a commercially favourable position.

We quickly decided, however, that this was not a business we were interested in pursuing, as we found that the time taken in counting the cash and processing it in high volumes used up resources that were better utilized in other places. We decided that we were better off focusing on our core offering.

However, this incident prompted us to ask ourselves if there were other similar situations where we found ourselves with a certain competitive edge, which we actually did want to take advantage of. It also encouraged us to search proactively for any trends, triggers or incidents that might have disrupted market forces, and which we could make use of.

In normal times, the market forces in play are almost visible to everyone involved: your competitors, your clients and other stake-holders. In times of crisis, disruptions take place. Exceptional market forces are in play, meaning that not all players are now seeing eye-to-eye on the market particulars. Not everyone is also bold enough to venture into new initiatives. In our case, some banks stopped lending, while others clamped down on their operations. We saw a growing reluctance amongst our competitors, amidst an increased uncertainty of the context, plagued by unpredictable client behaviour. This created overall inertia in the market. Not everyone pursues opportunities in such circumstances, as we saw in the previous chapter, because the instinctive reaction was to become more sluggish and conservative. It becomes harder for everyone to establish the clarity of their direction, and their actions become less definitive and more impulsive.

This is why this could be the optimal time for you to make a profound difference in the competitive landscape.

When people used to ask me in Syria how well we were doing, I would tell them that during the war we acquired certain strategic strengths that we were able to sustain far more effectively than we could in normal times.

Redefine your Critical Success Factors

At the outset of adverse times, structural changes can take place in the industry and among competitors. In some cases, this drastically alters the competitive landscape. In Syria, the dynamics of the competitive industry were transformed due to several factors. In times of crisis, it is essential that you are able to identify quickly these factors shaping the competitive landscape.

Success in any industry depends upon a company's ability to excel at certain factors related to that industry, which I have referred to earlier as the Critical Success Factors (CSFs). In adverse times, with changes taking place across many aspects of the industry, some of these CSFs are likely to get redefined, with some becoming more critical whereas others become less critical.

In Syria, for example, having enough liquidity before the war was theoretically a CSF in the banking industry, but since it was relatively easy to achieve, it was not so critical from a competitive perspective. Liquidity was always high in the market, and all banks were highly liquid, considering both the legally required ratios and best practices. As long as a bank was liquid above a certain threshold, being even more liquid did not give that bank much advantage; as such, it was not something that could be used to create a strategic rift amongst competitors before the war.

During the war, however, and with increasing withdrawals, liquidity became a scarce resource, which was not the case previously. When a bank is illiquid, it is unable to satisfy the growing requests for cash for its deposits. To attract more cash in the form of deposits, it will most likely resort to paying higher interest rates on its deposits. The bank in this case enters a cycle whereby it is losing liquidity and at the same time increasing its interest expenses on the deposits it is trying to attract. This makes it less able to lend money and, when able to lend, more likely to charge higher rates than before, to make up for the coupled increase in the interest expense. Therefore being illiquid has triggered a series of events for this bank in this situation, which has made it much more difficult for it to remain competitive. A more liquid bank would be better able to satisfy the growing need for cash and to safeguard its position, and would not be forced to increase the interest rate it charges on its deposits to attract significantly more deposits. This would enable this bank to lend at rates that are likely more competitive than those of the less liquid banks.

In the above example, liquidity suddenly becomes an integral element in competition, which unleashes a ripple effect across the competitiveness of the banks in play. Having high liquidity becomes a much more Critical Success Factor, and sustaining this becomes both more difficult and more fundamental to being able to compete in the market. Only by ensuring high liquidity can a bank sustain the capability to lend in high amounts and at competitive rates.

By analysing the criticality of each of our CSFs, at BBSF we reached the conclusion early on that we always had to ensure that we enhanced our capability to lend money and to have the lowest cost of funds. Any other ratio or metric, no matter how important, was secondary to this. We were highly focused on the redefined CSFs and did not overwhelm ourselves with plenty of other metrics. By becoming the most fit in lending money competitively and having the lowest cost of funds in these difficult times, we were able to excel and create a wide strategic drift between us and our competitors. In normal times, creating such a wide gap would not have been possible, as no events could be so drastic as to induce radical changes concerning the competitiveness of banks. In such adverse times, however, such a transformation was possible.

For competitive analysis it becomes more important to analyse and assess such factors rather than the normally observed standard industry ratios. For example, analysing a bank's market share of deposits, which is done during normal times, is still important, but its importance is dwarfed vis-à-vis the need to identify the newly redefined CSFs and assess how each bank is doing in that regard. A bank may very well have a high market share, which might imply that it is doing well. But if you know that it scores low in the industry CSFs, this enables you to place it in a declining trend and conclude that its capability to sustain this market share has decreased.

Examining our CSFs was part of our strategy formulation exercise, which entailed using Porter's Five Forces Model for our competitive analysis and developing a strategy map (see page 57). We found that the deliverables of this exercise enabled us to clearly identify the changing competitive landscape and what it takes to soar throughout disruption, and the concise strategy map ensured that we had greater visibility and clarity of direction amidst uncertain times.

Understand the changing competitive landscape through Porter's Five Forces Model

There are many methodologies, or frameworks, used in competitive analysis. I have found Porter's Five Forces Model, developed by the American academic Michael Porter, to be the most effective for us in our context. Counter-arguments usually state that dynamic industries change so fast that the conclusions derived from using this model will be seen as irrelevant at the end of the study. Some changes are indeed very dynamic; and analysis using Porter's Five Forces Model may need to be repeated more than once, whenever significant structural changes take place in the competitive arena; but the increasingly challenging situation should not simply lead to the discarding of an entire model that many find adept at assessing competitiveness. I believe that the process of competitive analysis – regardless of the model or tool used – should not be seen as a static one, especially in a crisis, as adjustments should be made when necessary and parts of the exercise repeated whenever significant new forces come into play. This is likely to happen much more often in difficult times.

We found it useful to ask ourselves the following questions in each of the five areas shown on the next page. Perhaps you can ask yourself these same questions, as part of the Porter's Five Forces Model assessment:

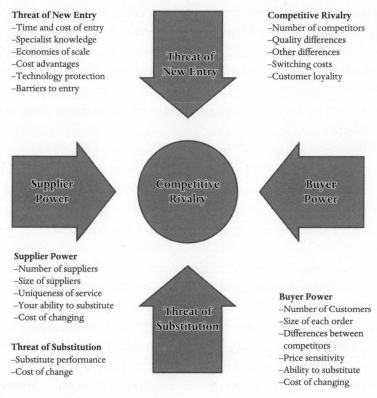

Threat of New Entry
–Time and cost of entry
–Specialist knowledge
–Economies of scale
–Cost advantages
–Technology protection
–Barriers to entry

Competitive Rivalry
–Number of competitors
–Quality differences
–Other differences
–Switching costs
–Customer loyality

Supplier Power
–Number of suppliers
–Size of suppliers
–Uniqueness of service
–Your ability to substitute
–Cost of changing

Threat of Substitution
–Substitute performance
–Cost of change

Buyer Power
–Number of Customers
–Size of each order
–Differences between
  competitors
–Price sensitivity
–Ability to substitute
–Cost of changing

Figure 1: Porter's Five Forces Model

Competitive Rivalry

What cost does my client incur to switch from my product/service to another (referred to as switching cost)? If it is low, how can I make it higher? If I have little control over the cost, how can I make it more difficult for my client to switch to another product/service? What is different in the market today that could make my client switch to a competitor? What features can I add to my product/service to make switching more difficult?

In banking, the switching cost for depositors is almost nil. Any client can simply close their account at one bank and open an account in another bank. Although this makes it easier for a bank to acquire its competitors' clients, it makes it more difficult to retain its own clients. However, banks can make it more difficult for clients to switch accounts. By adding in more services to a client that 'lock them in' (such as domiciling their telecom and utility bills with direct-debit features, and convincing them to invest in longer-term deposits), it becomes more difficult for this client to leave the bank. When a client becomes happily 'anchored', it becomes more difficult for them to switch. As such, even in cases where there are no apparent switching costs, there are areas in which you can create switching difficulties. Having said all that, you should not of course be anchoring your client through an imprisoning or coercing mindset, but rather by creating needs and satisfying them in a way in which the client find themselves happily 'attached'.

How do I measure the size and state of my competitors? Is the same set of criteria used previously still relevant now? How have adverse times affected them? Have some criteria become more important than others? Is it now a question of the number of branches? Or is it market share? Or total sales? How correlated are the new metrics to the newly redefined CSFs?

Before the crisis, we were analysing the conventional metrics, including assessing the market share of bank loans and deposits. But during the crisis these criteria became less relevant. According to the newly redefined CSFs, as discussed earlier, we identified that analysing our competitors' capability to lend competitively was one of the most important metrics to analyse – far more so than its actual market share. We started to analyse banks based on their liquidity and cost of funds (the interest expense paid on their deposits) and correlated this with their organic growth in loans. This was far from being a standard analysis, but it enabled us to focus on what mattered most: determining which banks were able to lend more competitively than others.

In banking there is very little differentiation when it comes to loans; at the end of the day, the customer is getting the same money whether it is from Bank A or Bank B. The interest rate charged remains almost the only determinant for differentiation. As such, price is essential, and being able to price competitively is a CSF. The start of the war forced illiquid banks to charge more in order to attract more deposits, thus making them less able to lend competitively. In adverse times it becomes more difficult for competitors to catch up. Once a strategic rift takes place, the ability to overcome it becomes tougher. Several banks in Syria that became illiquid got caught up in the vicious cycle of illiquidity. Not being liquid meant they could not always meet their cash-withdrawal needs, thus leading to a tarnishing of their reputation. They got stuck in this position and were unable to bypass it. Adverse times can reinforce polarized positions, because only the ones that are able to adapt quickly can flourish. Others will find themselves becoming increasingly uncompetitive and intrinsically unable to fulfil their CSFs. Anything else they do will not matter.

What are the new trends in place today? How has the crisis changed the context? What new products and services can be offered to differentiate ourselves from the competition? How good are we, compared with our competitors, in differentiating them?

This question takes us back to the incident where we found ourselves in a favourable position to transfer cash across the country.

Threat of New Entry

Do the main players in your industry have some form of first-mover advantage (derived from being first to operate in an industry)? Does being first come with certain sustainable advantages over the others? Have barriers to entry increased or decreased during these adverse times? What can you do to build even more barriers to entry, thus making it harder and less appealing for others to tap into your market?

This was less relevant in our case, as there was no threat of new banks entering the market. As a matter of fact Syria was poised for a number of regional banks to open that particular year when the troubles began and the following year, but they all ended up freezing their plans.

Do you have certain staff and technology that constitute CSFs in this industry? Has the crisis made them more in demand in the market? If yes, then how are you safeguarding them and making use of them?

We had a sophisticated technology infrastructure that linked together all our branches across the country. Many banks, including ourselves, naturally had their main connectivity nodes near the central city of Homs before the war, which made sense from an infrastructural point of view. However, when Homs became the epicentre of the conflict early on, this posed problems. All banks faced the same systematic security escalations on the ground as we did, and this we could not change. What we could create, however – and did – was a readjustment of our technology platforms. Early on in the crisis we reconfigured the infrastructure in such a way that it resembled a 'star-shaped' structure, which (as the name implies) joins several connector points with each other, thus decreasing dependence on the central nodes. This changed the way we operated so that we became less dependent on a small number of central nodes where a breakout in one would affect the entire network. This ensured that we were more capable than other banks to create connectivity amongst our branches, so that in many instances our ATMs worked in far-away cities more than those of other banks. Ensuring connectivity amongst the work of our branches became more of a critical factor during the war, because before the war all banks could more or less easily ensure that their technology platform worked efficiently; but less so during the war.

Supplier Power

Who are your main suppliers? Who is at risk of going out of business in such adverse times? If all your suppliers stop supplying you tomorrow, what can you do? Do you have alternative suppliers?

By nature I am not a hoarder. But early on we had to do more hoarding in the bank than we were ever used to. There was the risk of suppliers going out of business and the risk of currency depreciation, and therefore an almost definitive increase in prices on the horizon, especially for items that did not originate in Syria.

We made a list of all the non-perishable items that the bank usually purchased, from stationery to ATM paper rolls to printer ink, and anything else you can imagine that banks use. We stockpiled. This locked in a favourable price for us and ensured that we did not take supplier risk, as now we were able to get ATM paper rolls; it would not be so certain in a year or so, though.

It becomes important to identify the suppliers that could become strategic partners in adverse times. These suppliers might hold the supply of resources that are likely to become scarce in times of crisis. In Syria, our suppliers of diesel and water suddenly became the most important and sought-after suppliers for us. In the past these commodities were plentiful and were not considered strategic at all. The crisis changed all this. We ensured that we took better care of managing our relationships with these suppliers.

A study should be made of the main resources that you need for your business to proceed in an uninterrupted manner, and you should assess their scarcity, their growing criticality and the number of suppliers involved in them. From there, you will be able to determine how best to ensure that you always have access to these supplies.

Threat of Substitution

What products/services were usually substituted for yours before the crisis? How have adverse times changed this? Are there any new emerging substitutes in the market? If yes, on what basis are they competing against your products/services? Would it be feasible – while avoiding product cannibalism – to sell this substitute product/service yourself? Have changing times created situations for you in other markets for your own products/services to act as substitutes for other products and services?

In the previous chapter I talked about how many people initially withdrew their money from banks in the run-ons. For those who did not return their deposits to us, we started asking: What will they do with this money? We knew some people would take their money abroad. Others were bound to hide it underneath their mattress, or exchange it into foreign currency. Many started buying gold or other valuables. We spotted an opportunity here – might people feel safer keeping these newly acquired valuables in safe-deposit boxes in banks rather than in their homes? We built state-of-the art safe-deposit boxes in all different sizes in our new headquarters in central Damascus. If we couldn't convince people to keep their savings with us in cash, then we could retain some of them as customers by offering an alternative way to safeguard their wealth in its new form.

Buyer Power

How powerful is your client in deciding to choose your product over another? How has the crisis changed this? Does the customer now have more or less buyer power? Is your product systematically more in demand, less in demand or the same in these adverse times?

In Damascus, buyers had the ultimate power when it came to drinking water. Tap water was mostly drinkable and almost free. There was virtually no market for sparkling water. Bottled water was plentiful, as many Syrian and Lebanese companies were active in this market.

As I wrote the first draft of this chapter, escalating physical violence led to damage to the main spring that supplied water to Damascus. There was limited tap water for a few weeks. A change in the market, due to adverse times, radically transformed buyer power there, from yielding immense power before the war to now yielding almost none. Water became very scarce, and bottles soared so high in price that it became utterly ridiculous. There are no substitutes for water, and demand for it has remained unchanged. This is an extreme example that you will hopefully never face, but it illustrates how changes in adverse times can radically alter buying power. You should keep an eye out for these changes and be able to address them proactively and swiftly to improve your competitiveness.

After we had completed our competitive analysis using Porter's Five Forces Model, it was time to decide on what to do and what to focus upon. We came up with a one-page strategy map.

Focus on what matters

In times of crisis, you are bound to get drawn into the distressing daily challenges that you will face. Operational and tactical difficulties will arise from both known and unknown sources, forcing you to exert much effort in resolving these issues. It will become easy to get swept away by these challenges in such a way that you slowly start to lose focus on the bigger picture. Resolving these increasingly difficult daily challenges is of the utmost importance, and ensuring that the actions you take are well aligned with your overall corporate strategy is also highly significant.

The formulation of a corporate strategy is vital, even more so in a crisis. Having a clear vision of what your company aspires to achieve, in light of this changing context, is fundamental; it provides clarity, purpose and direction in an otherwise chaotic time. In unsettled times, the room for misunderstanding, miscommunication and disorientation grows. Many of your people might become lost and confused and start to question the very basic tenets of your company. You might decide to close a certain branch or point of sale, from an operational challenge or difficulty; some of your staff might interpret this as the first step before complete withdrawal. They will start to wonder whether you are clamping down on your services, and could interpret this as a strategic down-sizing initiative.

Confusion easily arises, because times of crisis provide fertile ground for the emergence of 'conspiracy theories', unconstructive chatter and further drifting into the oblivion of the unknown.

The act of formulating a corporate strategy is undertaken differently by different companies. For some, strategic planning is undertaken as part of a distinctly well-defined function, and follows a conventional top-down rational approach. In other companies, strategic development falls under a pattern normally defined as freewheeling opportunism, where no formal planning is undertaken per se, but rather opportunities and strategies are pursued based on the changes in the prevailing market. In other companies, an incremental approach is pursued, whereby incremental changes are made to the strategy, based on the evolution of events. There is no right or wrong approach; the process of defining and pursuing a strategy depends on many factors, most importantly the culture of the company, its industry and the overlying context.

I have found that in adverse times the need to establish clarity and purpose over all areas gains greater importance, and the more structured and focused the approach in doing so, the more you will be able to develop an effective strategy that will provide the clarity and direction you seek.

Some people argue that in a drastically changing context, strategic development becomes less important. Here it becomes important to distinguish between corporate strategy and tactics.

A corporate strategy relates to the overall direction of the company. A company should have corporate strategic objectives that it wishes to fulfil, regardless of the overlying context. So, for example, at BBSF our vision was to become the number-one bank for all Syrians. One of the strategic objectives that we defined was to become the best employer in Syria. This has been upheld as a corporate strategic objective, regardless of the development of the context. In bad times or good, the company has committed itself to this objective because it has a belief that by achieving this, it will take a step towards fulfilling its overall vision. Now achieving this strategic objective requires several tactics. And it is these tactics that will be susceptible to change, due to the changing environment. Perhaps in normal times grouping all our staff in a monthly training session over a weekend was a tactic that was used. In war, this became impossible, and so different tactics were used. But the overall corporate strategic objective remained the same; the context entailed a change in the tactic, but not in the strategic objective. Having said that, the escalation of events in a crisis may prompt you to alter your strategic objectives in some instances, but this should not be viewed as a frequent thing, but rather as an acceptance of the need to be flexible and continuously dynamic and receptive to change.

No matter what methodology you use, the important thing is that you end up developing a one-page strategy map at the outset of the crisis. After having engaged in the Porter's Five Forces Model analysis, as laid out earlier, you will have developed a more rigorous understanding of the transformation of the competitive landscape. Now comes the time to conduct a strategic analysis that identifies your main strengths and weaknesses, and that relates them to the overall context. Trends need to be identified, along with their implications to your business. A SWOT analysis could be used to analyse your internal characteristics, enabling you to determine and clearly define your **S**trengths, **W**eaknesses, **O**pportunities unfolding with the crisis and the **T**hreats that increasingly come your way.

Ultimately a one-page strategy map should have not more than four headings, as follows:

- Vision
- Strategic objectives
- Tactics
- Overriding values and business principles

Everything stems from the *vision*. You should be able to develop a one-sentence vision that explains what your company aspires to achieve. It should be inspirational and should incorporate elements that are presently not fulfilled, thus providing a motivating zeal for the company to fulfil. Our vision was simply to become the number-one bank for all Syrians.

Some will argue that a mission statement explains the 'what' and 'who' of a company and needs to be developed first, whereas the vision needs to explain the 'why' and 'how' of the company's mission statement. You can do that, of course. We found that over-complicating different notions in adverse times could provide less clarity, rather than more. Having a single vision, followed by not more than five *strategic objectives*, can more easily be reinforced and established in the mindsets of people and will provide them with the clarity they need.

The extent to which there is alignment between the strategic objectives and the actual actions undertaken is of the utmost importance – far more so than the articulation and distinction between vision, mission statement, corporate strategy, business strategy, and so on. The fewer terms and definitions you use, the more fluid your strategy becomes and the easier it is for your people to understand. People need a coherent, concise and logical story to follow, especially in a crisis; unlike some MBA professors, they won't lose their minds if you include parts of your mission statement under 'vision'.

The strategic objectives should in principle work towards satisfying the vision. The *tactics* explain the 'how to' element. These are changeable and can be revised when necessary. They explain what actions need to be taken (with one sentence for each tactic) to ensure the fulfilment of the strategic objective. As a rule of thumb, I would not recommend developing more than five tactics for each strategic objective.

Finally, a set of not more than five *overriding values and business principles* should be developed that govern the overall ethics and code of conduct expected from your company. Setting the ethical compass is important, so that your people become aware of the established values of your company. If these have been already set, then a possible revision can be considered to see what values are more relevant and important now. Because in principle values should not be subjected to much change, what can be done is to highlight, for example, certain examples of fulfilment of these values that are more related to the context of the crisis.

Try not to develop more than five objectives, five values and five tactics for each objective. It becomes very tempting, and actually very easy, to develop as many of these as possible. The aim, however, is to be focused and confined to the supreme priorities of the company; this will greatly enhance the necessary clarity and direction in difficult times.

Now that a competitive analysis has been made and a focused strategy developed, it is up to the leadership to ensure that what is being planned is executed. I have found that a distinct type of leadership works best in a crisis: situational leadership. This takes us to the next chapter, but first here are some questions to ask yourself to help you create a strategic rift in a crisis:

- No one likes a crisis – but if it is unavoidable, how can you proactively face it?
- How are the CSFs of the industry being redefined? Which of these factors are becoming more critical? How are you responding to these dynamically changing CSFs?
- Can a competitive assessment model, such as Porter's Five Forces Model, help you? (Please refer to page 49 for the relevant section in this chapter for more specific questions concerning the model's different elements.)
- As you are drawn into the distressing daily challenges of a crisis, what are you doing to achieve greater clarity, purpose and direction?
- If you had to come up with a one-page strategy map, how would you highlight your brief vision, a few strategic objectives, tactics and values?

5

Be a situational leader

Glorified leadership and false dichotomy

When first visiting the Middle East, outsiders are typically struck by one particular thing upon arrival: the oversized posters of presidents, kings and emirs scattered everywhere – on street billboards, on the walls of narrow alleys and even inside chickpea eateries. Leaders have always been glorified and given illustrious status in the Middle East, from Egyptian pharaohs, Babylonian kings and the princes of different Arabian dynasties to the heads of state of modern times. This is not to say that this radical view trickles down to encompass leadership in all other aspects of life, such as within families and in the workplace, but it does slightly. In varying degrees across different subcultures and social contexts, leaders are to some extent supposed to be unchallenged, uncompromising and do not take a step backwards. They do not admit mistakes. Followers tend to always to praise their leaders, feeding into their egos and, in doing so, create in them a continuously growing inflated sense of self-esteem. Leaders are inclined to feel that people have the choice of either loving them or fearing them, and they most often choose the latter.

This brings us to the deeply engrained trait in the critical thinking process of the Arab psyche: the fallacy of false dichotomy. Things, options and alternatives can be either black or white. In Syria, your political view, for example, is typically categorized as being either 'pro' or 'anti' and each label carries within it a ton of prejudices. Try to have your own individual opinion of things, advocating and criticizing some aspects of both camps, and most people will view you as unprincipled and 'grey', a word that carries negative connotations. Being called 'grey' is a curse in the Middle East – one of the more emphatic ones actually. 'Grey' people are demonized by those who adhere uncritically to their alleged notions of black and white.

False dichotomy is a logical fallacy because flawed reasoning is used to arrive at the conclusion that there are only two alternatives to a given situation. This type of thinking permeates its way throughout social and even corporate subcultures, so that people, concepts and styles *have* to be labelled as belonging to one of two groupings. A leader is considered to have *only two* options – to be either autocratic or democratic – as this simplistic categorization falls within the conventional framework of identifying different possibilities. If a leader can be both, this then becomes harder to assess, harder to categorize and, as such, harder to accept as a plausible option.

In a crisis, this creates a problem. With this notion of glorified leadership and with increased praise in tough times, leaders are granted a false sense of superiority, which elevates them from the ground at a time when they actually need to have an improved ability to be affixed to the ground and more in touch with reality. Moreover, as crisis leads to an abundance of varying spectrums of possible decisions to take, potential turns of events and factors to consider, an enhanced sense of judgement is required to assess all the possible options. All this becomes even more difficult to implement when being crippled by the prevalent flawed sense of reasoning that sees choices as one of two options.

Leadership: back to basics

Let's take a step backwards and see what leadership is meant to be about. There are many schools of thought that lay down what it takes to ensure effective leadership. Because leadership is an abstract term, it becomes easy to manoeuvre around it using different concepts. Some claim that charisma is essential, while others disagree. Some think it is better to take time to make decisions, while others say that decisions should be taken fast. Some advocate certain leadership styles, while others believe in the presence of a wide spectrum of acceptable styles. Leadership is a very fluid term, and academics and emerging *smart thinkers* love to augment it continually with new dimensions. You can rest assured that I will not be 'inventing' a new leadership model.

Let's analyse the basics. In both normal and adverse times, people need clarity, purpose and direction, as discussed in the previous chapter. In normal times with steady environments, some businesses may succeed without exerting much effort in providing these three elements. Sometimes the business dynamics are simple enough to be self-evident, in the sense that not much is required to explain the purpose and direction. In all situations, however, successful companies must provide some form of clarity as to what they are about.

In adverse times there is greater uncertainty. People will be less orientated towards corporate purpose and there will be less visibility. So the need to make things clearer and to provide direction becomes more important. There will be instances when fast decisions need to be taken in volatile times, prompting a more central decision-making approach. On the other hand, there are also instances when someone needs to take a step back and, despite the temptation of everyone around them to 'force' a decision 'right now', they will decide to take the necessary time to consider all the aspects before deciding what to do. So what is one of the most important, unique skill sets of leading in a crisis?

BBSF has had six different CEOs in eight years since the crisis started in early 2011. Each one of them was so different from the others. One spent all day in the office, while another was always outside, meeting clients. Whereas one loved reading reports and sent almost a hundred emails a day, another never sent an email. One was interested in constantly making internal corporate changes, while another focused solely on customers. A CEO's actions mould the priorities of the company's operations, whether or not they talk about it explicitly. Their leadership style determines a large part of their actions. I believe that the turnover of CEOs we had at the bank was due partly to some of them being less able to be situational – that is, to change their style depending on the situation. By being confined in their approach, they found living up to the challenges of a crisis difficult.

By seeing the best and worst in each of those CEOs with whom I worked closely in a developing crisis with serious implications (I worked with four of these six CEOs), and by reflecting on my own style over these years, I learned the importance of knowing that the course of action to be taken in a crisis depends on the situation. It might sound like a very basic thing, but in a crisis with changing contexts and variables, and in a culture where glorified leadership and false dichotomy prevail, the capacity for a leader to be able to assess each situation with its own specifics, and be willing to have the open-mindedness to take decisions differently from one situation to another, is a very difficult trait to possess.

Situational leadership

There are many leadership styles, one of which is the autocratic style whereby the leader takes all the decisions themselves. At the other end of the spectrum is the participatory style, which involves as many people as possible in the decision-making process. Numerous discussions have taken place on the effectiveness of each style and on the different situations they should be used in. Kenneth Blanchard and Paul Hersey devised the infamous Situational Leadership model, which in essence states that each situation requires a different leadership style. The model argues that the unique dynamics of each situation govern the choice of leadership style. Advocating an absolute style does not work, because different contexts necessitate different approaches.

In times of crisis, the conventional recommendation is that an autocratic approach is most appropriate, as it assures that fast decisions are taken by the leader. But this assumes a situation where there is a well-defined crisis within a short period. In prolonged times of crisis, it all becomes a little trickier. I worked in Syria during unrest for more than four years; all in all, this entire period can be considered 'extremely adverse'. However, we were not operating in a one-off crisis with a confined time limit that required immediate decisions to be taken at all times. In one instance a mortar bomb hit the bank's headquarters while I was there and this sparked a real immediate crisis, with immediate risks to our lives. At other times, things and processes flowed quite normally. So even though we worked during war in the macro sense, in the micro aspect of things not every day entailed working in a warlike environment that required an autocratic leadership approach. Being fixated on adopting an absolute style based on the macro picture can become confining.

In a crisis successful situational leaders have the capacity to engage in a wide spectrum of varying actions and get five things right:

1. Strategic, yet always on the ground
2. Persistent, yet knowing when to stop digging
3. Focused, but not restrained
4. Adaptive, yet not submissive in stakeholder management
5. Leading change, but not changing everything.

1 Strategic, yet always on the ground

An earlier chapter emphasized the importance of always being aware of the overall vision and working towards fulfilling the strategic objectives of the organization. A leader needs to provide clarity, purpose and direction in an increasingly shadowy setting. Yet that does not mean that a leader should stay aloof and disconnected from what is going on, on the ground.

Early on in the war I was given the temporary assignment of being in charge of operations and was entrusted with the task of revamping the effectiveness of the cash-counting duties of the bank tellers. I made an elementary mistake in assuming that the average deposit of one million Syrian pounds would most likely come in banknotes of 1,000 pounds – the highest banknote denomination back then. It was an honest assumption, on my behalf, just as you would imagine that a million-dollar withdrawal would comprise stacks of 100-dollar bills. But I should have known better. In reality, and due mainly to inflation and Central Bank interference in the injection of cash, these banknotes became increasingly rare, and banknotes of much smaller denomination became more common. Depositing one million Syrian pounds back then would take place most of the time in banknotes of 200 Syrian pounds, instead of the 1,000 denomination that I assumed. This was not something I had known, in my position. This meant that the bank teller had five times as many banknotes to handle as my study assumed – rendering it useless. This simple observation was elementary to any junior teller in the bank, but not to me, as a senior manager.

In times of crisis, the situation on the ground might evolve to be very different from your own perspective, if you are not in touch with what is going on. Increasing the involvement in the decision-making process of the very people on the ground will become more essential, when it comes to tactics and operations. Seek the advice of your part-time security guard to give you a recommendation on how best to revamp the security of your premises, in addition to seeking the advice of whoever is in charge of those operations. Senior managers sitting aloof in their offices will use their knowledge of best practice and policies and procedures to make decisions. Your security guard – given that he spends the whole day eyeing the premises – will have identified anomalies and gaps that these managers have probably never seen.

Adverse times lead to divergent behaviour and the emergence of unusual occurrences that can only be identified by those on the ground. Adverse times can instil small changes across your business cycle that will not necessarily be visible to your managers. After this incident, I learned from my mistake and ensured that I involved teams on the ground in all decisions that affected their tactical operations. Even the cleaning man can sometimes surprise you, with what a non-specialist can see. Creating small task forces composed of people on the ground to recommend solutions in adverse times was very effective. These staff became more motivated, as they felt more involved and, ultimately, had a genuine need for their problems to be resolved in order to make things easier for them. In many instances, companies give back-office people the job of improving the work of front-office people. This frustrates front-office people so much, because they are the ones facing the increasing difficulties and know best how to resolve them. Imagine how furious an accountant would be if a salesperson was entrusted with changing the depreciation rates used in the bookkeeping process. The same applies to your front-office staff. They have to be involved, to improve your understanding of what is happening on the ground. Listen to even the most junior staff; there will be much insight to gain. A situational leader in a crisis knows when to be on the ground, and encourages managers to become closer to the ground; they know they might be far off from correctly perceiving the way things actually work if they don't.

Involving all parties in making recommendations is not synonymous with empowering them to make the decisions themselves. An excellent leader in adverse times is capable of effectively involving and engaging their staff in decisions, and is able to separate this process from the actual decision-making process.

A good leader in a crisis has the capacity to know when to get down to the gritty details on the ground and empower people, but at the same time when to stay afloat and not allow themselves to drown amidst the daily challenges. Their occasional closer involvement on the ground does not compromise their strategic perspective. As the gritty details become grittier, it becomes tempting for a leader to stay afloat, leaving the 'dirty' jobs to those beneath them. But successful leaders in a crisis know that it's not only about planning or execution, but almost always about both. They also know that the degree of their involvement in the planning and execution depends on the actual situation. They are able to make that judgement as the situation evolves, and do not let themselves become fixated on an absolutist approach.

2 Persistent, yet knowing when to stop digging

A successful situational leader is persistent and relentless in their pursuits – a theme that is repeated and elaborated on throughout this book. They are, however, consciously aware that excessive persistence might be reckless and may cause more harm than good. Venturing on unrealistically, without the right tools or an understanding of the context and the underlying factors, can be a recipe for disaster. Persistence does not mean committing blindly to a certain route if it simply does not work.

Managing in a crisis is a novel experience for most people. There is a learning curve involved, just as there is for everything else in life. You are bound to make mistakes. I know I made many – such as the time I misjudged the assumptions in my cash-counting study. In a crisis, it is likely that you may find yourself in a hole you have dug yourself. It is essential that an environment that accepts mistakes, and actually cherishes learning from them, is encouraged. No vindication should be made, or else a culture of blame and villainization will emerge that will sap morale. As the context changes, clashes will become inevitable, as old modes of action will seem unable to meet the demands of new experiences.

An excellent leader is someone who is tolerant of mistakes and is able to learn from them. When they find themselves in a hole, they do not dig themselves deeper. They have the sense of judgement to be able to assess whether this is indeed a hole that needs to be exited from as soon as possible. They have the courage to admit failure in this particular aspect or area and to get out of the hole, accepting the cost entailed. Excellent leaders do not derive their self-worth from the commitment of such mistakes. They cherish mistakes and make sure that lessons are learned.

You will revamp your policies and procedures to combat new challenges, only to find that they did not work out the way you wanted them to. That's okay. Excellent leaders have the audacity to revert to the way things were, when necessary, or to pursue other alternatives. There is no shame in that. They also have the aptitude to learn from others' experiences, which is much harder than learning from your own. They will be well informed on changes that are occurring in the current context and market, and on what actions competitors took. If some of these actions taken by competitors failed, then effective leaders will analyse what went wrong and deliberate on how this learning experience can be transferable to their own organization.

3 Focused, but not restrained

Focus is key, as discussed in the previous chapter. It becomes easy and tempting to get distracted in a crisis, when you have to deal with continually emerging issues and challenges across all levels. Many things break down, so even more things will need attention now. Things that were taken for granted will now need continuous assessment. Risks that did not even exist will emerge.

Before the war we never had to worry too much about security at BBSF. Syria was a very safe country with virtually no organized crime, minimal homicide and almost no bank robberies. When we and other banks transported cash between branches, we applied procedures that might appear lax, compared to the way cash between bank branches is transported in cities like Zurich and London. Suddenly all of this changed. In addition to the increasing challenges we faced, we had to solve problems by significantly enhancing our security. Some people I meet in London view the

Middle East as a homogeneous territory, and think that just by living there one is used to a 'war mentality', but this is not the case. I felt safer in Damascus before the war than I felt anywhere else in the world. We had very little experience of enhancing security, and found ourselves needing to re-examine many of the tasks that we ordinarily did and took for granted.

Difficulty arises when, after having identified the CSFs (see page 21) and what areas you need to focus and work on, operational challenges keep emerging. You suddenly have to juggle 'too many watermelons', as a Syrian proverb strongly advises against. If you do juggle all of them, some watermelons are bound to drop, and no one likes to deal with a broken watermelon.

The challenge is always keeping an eye on the strategic focus and vision. There are two risks associated with this. If you allow yourself to do too many things, then you risk losing sight of your strategic focus. If you are too focused and decide to do only a few things because 'these matter the most', then you may be inattentive to aspects that are operationally or tactically essential. Being focused does not free you from addressing the challenges, or from limiting the scope of your awareness. This becomes even more difficult as a crisis expands, with new factors emerging and new events unfolding. The most successful leader in a crisis is able to stay focused, but does not allow this focus to restrain their scope.

4 Adaptive, yet not submissive in stakeholder management

When a crisis unfolds, people's needs change. This includes the needs of your customers, staff, suppliers, shareholders, regulators and others. You can rest assured that they will almost always become more demanding, rather than less. Almost everything will become 'urgent' and 'important'. Some of these changing needs will be driven by emotional factors, others by more rational ones. Some stem from purely individual motives, while others pertain to organizational needs.

A successful situational leader knows that there is no black-and-white solution here. Each situation is particular. Sometimes you will need to appeal to emotion, while at other times you will need to appeal to more rational factors. When everyone is vying for attention regarding their most 'urgent' issue, the ability to assess the urgency of each situation based on *your* priorities becomes even more important. When everyone is pressing you to make a decision now, you should be able to listen, but not get carried away. Say yes to all decisions, and you will unleash a barrage of more requests and demands for attention, and you cannot possibly say yes to all of them. Say no to everything, and you will definitely be risking your relationship with key people who affect your organization. Decide on everything at the moment, and you risk having made a hasty decision based on an incomplete set of variables. Postpone all decisions by embracing a more meticulous decision-making process, and you risk hampering your ability to take decisions in a fast-paced environment with increasing challenges.

In light of all these options, what you should do really depends on the situation. A successful leader in a crisis is conscious of this process. Know your priorities and your readily available tools, as well as the time that you have to commit to changing needs. Show empathy at all times and, most importantly, orientate your stakeholders' priorities and urgencies to your organization's needs, rather than changing your own to match theirs. In all circumstances, make sure you keep excellent relations with all stakeholders and that you are fair. Enhance your ability to really understand their evolving needs. If you can't do what is asked of you, then by understanding their evolving needs and what this entails you have a better chance of doing something else that may perhaps partially satisfy them.

Strong empathy, a conscious awareness of why people's needs are evolving and a robust judgement of what matters, and what should be done, should guide you to be adaptive in your stakeholder management, without being either submissive or apathetic to changing needs.

5 Leading change, but not changing everything

This is one of the most essential qualities of a successful situational leader. I believe it is so important that I have dedicated the entire next chapter to it, as it represents a main principle in managing in a crisis.

First here are some questions to ask yourself to help you become a better situational leader in a crisis:

- With increasing uncertainty in a crisis, how is your leadership providing greater clarity, purpose and direction?
- If you are in crisis at the macro level, do you allow this to prevent you from objectively assessing the micro view of things? Is your macro view muddling your vision?
- What might you miss out on, if you stay disconnected from the ground? What might happen to your strategic direction if you get too close to the ground? How can you find the right balance between the two?
- Is managing in a crisis a novel experience for you and your people? How accepting are you of mistakes? What do you do when you find yourself in a hole? Do you think it represents positive persistence if you commit to a certain route, even if it simply does not work? Could an intentional retreat work better?
- Are you driven by your strategic focus and vision? Does your increased focus restrain you from doing the things that matter on the ground? Is your focus restraining your scope?
- As your stakeholders become more demanding, how can you maintain focus on your own priorities and urgencies? How can you show sympathy without being submissive?

6

Change, but don't rush to change everything

The importance of assessing the need for change

The notion of change has become so all-pervasive that everyone seems to be employing it. Engrossed in the belief that what is old is obsolete or has become increasingly irrelevant, everyone seems to want to keep on changing everything, both in themselves and around them. With clichés and popular wisdom bombarding people and organizations with the pressure to change, you may feel guilty if you are not changing in one way or another. Change that enables you to keep up more effectively with the growing challenges and emerging requirements is good, but it becomes problematic when it is made just for the sake of it.

In a crisis, it will be even more tempting to call for change. As the context alters dramatically, many systems and arrangements already in place will seem less capable of facing the incoming challenges. Things will sometimes seem to fall apart, so the need to not only introduce change, but engage in transformation, may emerge as one of the only plausible means on hand to confront new challenges.

The fact that transformation will be required in many different aspects does not mean that everything in a crisis will require change. As I mentioned earlier, we had six different CEOs at BBSF over a period of eight years. Most newcomers are induced by nature to deviate from the way things were done before, and attempt to effect changes as profound as possible to mark their presence and distinguish them from their predecessor. The overriding message that every newcomer wishes to relay seems to be one of 'Now *this* is how things should be done.' With six different CEOs reigning in a short period with varying styles, the barrage of changes to which the bank was subjected was immense.

One of the most important general qualities of leadership is the ability to lead a change process. There is much literature covering the optimal way to lead change, and it lies rather outside the scope of this book. What I am most concerned with is the additional, and perhaps equally difficult, competence that becomes of paramount importance in difficult times: the capability to assess the *need* for change. When you steer a boat in a storm you need to adjust the sail and mast every once in a while, but rocking it with too many adjustments could lead to an ill-fated downfall.

An effective leader in a crisis recognizes the unhealthy triggers of change and is capable of identifying areas that need transformation, but does not uproot core values. They have the unique capability to identify the need for, and extent of, change. They usually get four things right:

1. Being mindful of opposing forces in a changing context
2. Rewiring their thinking: from temporary and permanent changes, to changes mapped against the CSFs
3. Having a strong sense of the organization's core values
4. Always asking the 'five whys'.

1 Being mindful of opposing forces in a changing context

In a crisis there are opposing forces at play. The context is fast-paced and changing. New difficulties emerge that complicate work, raise uncertainty and generally make things harder for everyone involved. Change and deviation from the way things were done previously may be required in many areas. At the other end of the scale, when things are becoming more and more troublesome, people crave stability even more in adverse times. If they are to embrace change, they will probably be supportive only if it is clear that such change will make their lives easier in their everyday tasks.

Introducing change after change for the sake of it will simply destroy morale, at a time when you most need it.

An excellent leader in a crisis realizes that change can induce stress and, while they are willing to stress the system when necessary to do the right thing (as discussed in Chapter 1), they are mindful of these opposing forces and of the importance of not shocking the system unnecessarily. They reflect on the merits of the opposing forces and do not predispose themselves by default to follow a certain direction.

Our asset-liability management meetings at the bank, where we discussed liquidity issues and interest rates on deposits and loans, were quite boring before the war. We had comfortable liquidity levels, so the discussions weren't very exciting. Meetings would sometimes last for just ten minutes. At other times, we wouldn't even hold one. During the war such meetings became much more eventful and would sometimes last for a couple of hours. The chairperson now had to be mindful of two main camps, each with their own reasonable concerns and challenges. At one end, the back-office camp was worried that the cost of continuously paying high interest on deposits would hamper the bank's profitability. At the other end, the front-office camp would defend such tactics as a means to ensure greater liquidity. The timeless banking dilemma of liquidity versus profitability arose profoundly, each camp having its own merits. The successful leader here is one who is mindful of both opposing forces, who understands where everyone is coming from and who weighs carefully the pros and cons of each camp, before determining what change is needed.

2 Rewiring their thinking: from temporary and permanent changes, to changes mapped against the CSFs

As a general rule, in normal times across many workplaces, temporary measures are taken to face temporary challenges, and permanent measures or changes for permanent challenges. The difficulty that arises in a crisis is that it becomes much harder to draw the line between what is temporary and what is permanent.

When the war started in Syria, we had no idea whether many of the new challenges were temporary or not. It was not as if we faced new regulations, where all the parameters of the issue at hand were known to us and easy to define. The Syrian pound started to fluctuate. Many depositors withdrew their money. Security risks increased. Would it stop? Or would it become worse? How would things unfold? In such circumstances the line between temporary and permanent becomes so blurred that it is increasingly difficult to assess what kind of measure to take. Policies and procedures were generally developed to work in stable times, according to set assumptions. If some of those very assumptions are now being questioned, then how can they continue to remain relevant?

This takes us back to the earlier lessons about transforming your concept of time and playing the long game (see page 24). It becomes almost futile to engage in questions about how things will unfold; rather, attention should be paid to identifying the changing criticality of the industry's Critical Success Factors, and to ensuring that you are continuously able to meet them. The thinking approach should be less oriented towards being able to distinguish between temporary and permanent changes, to come up with the kind of change required, but rather more towards ensuring that your actions and change initiatives are continuously evolving, to be aligned with the evolving criticality of the industry's CSFs.

3 Having a strong sense of the organization's core values

Every organization has core values that represent main facets of its identity. Changing someone's behaviour linked to a habit is much more difficult than attempting to change a behaviour linked to a deeply embedded system of values and beliefs. The same applies to organizations.

There are core values in an organizational culture that have emerged for one reason or another, and which ensure or encourage that work gets done the way it does. These govern unwritten codes of behaviour or rules or style. Sometimes not only do these work, but the fact that they have grown organically and are embedded within the psyche of the staff means that these features of the culture can be a source of positivity in a crisis.

BBSF was always renowned as being more generous than other banks. This big-hearted approach concerning staff benefits was a core value. We were not wastefully lavish, but we were definitely not frugal, as some other banks were. We had a practice, from day one, whereby we normally paid salaries one month in advance. Why not? As a bank, we never had cashflow problems and the only risk came if an employee left during the subsequent month, in which case we would simply deduct their salary. It was a small, manageable risk. When someone started work, they would get paid at the end of the month, as they were still on probation. Once they were confirmed in the position three months later, they would get paid two salaries: one for the month they had just worked in and the other for the subsequent month. People really liked the way they got paid, and it didn't cost the bank much. During the crisis there was a serious suggestion in one of the meetings to cancel this, and to stop paying salaries in advance. This would mean that for one month we would skip paying the payroll, because salaries were paid up front. Yes, it would have slightly helped our cash position, but people would get furious. In the first place it was an exceptional arrangement, but with time it became the norm, and people planned their spending behaviour according to the payment timeline. Skipping a salary for a month in tough times would be challenging for people to cope with, even if that extra salary had in fact been paid in the past. This change would have affected the core value of being generous. Why do that? The cost would definitely outweigh the benefits. Thankfully, the decision was never made to skip paying a month's payroll.

Attempting to change areas that are closely associated with an organization's core values is immensely difficult in normal times, let alone in a crisis. An excellent leader in a crisis is strongly aware of their organization's core values and is careful not to engage in structural changes that negatively shake the organization where it hurts, and that affect its ability to engage in the necessary activities as prescribed by the evolving CSFs of the industry.

4 Always asking the 'five whys'

It's easy to get overwhelmed in a crisis. People have different needs. Some calls for change will be motivated by reasons that are not aligned with your organizational purposes. Others will be driven by the individual comfort of the people behind it, rather than by organizational necessity. There will be camps opposing change, and there will be people demanding that change is quick and that a decision is made right now. Others will attempt to delay the decision-making process behind a certain change.

A successful leader in a crisis asks the 'five whys' behind every change. It is a simple, yet very effective technique: when someone asks for something to be changed, ask 'Why?', then do that again four times following each response. This enables you to break down the problem and engage in a logical analytical process, to identify the *true* reason behind the need for change. Sometimes it even serves as a useful coaching technique to enable the other person to truly understand the real reasons behind their request, which might differ from what they initially thought. This enables you to carefully align what is requested with the current priorities mapped in the organization's strategy map. It enables you not to bend to pressure, or say yes or no indiscriminately.

By using a consistent methodical approach, people will become aware of the structured approach in assessing the need for change, and will be more diligent in making requests for change. This is important because in a crisis there will be numerous requests for change, and a successful leader is able to show that although they not only welcome change and embrace it, they ask the right questions and ensure that only what is required to change will do so.

The five outcomes of change

Eventually, when the extent and direction of change are identified, there are roughly five possible outcomes:

Good outcomes
1. Change to less
2. Change to more
3. Remain still

Bad outcomes
4. Remain passive – don't do anything
5. Change things half-heartedly.

Change is not always synonymous with 'doing more'. Sometimes it is about doing less of something, or restructuring it to be more adept at facing a new challenge. At the same time, you should not be confined to the 'less is more' mentality. Sometimes doing more innovatively is the response to change. At other times you may decide to remain still, which is a different response from remaining passive. Changing things half-heartedly is usually the result of too many decisions in a change process.

We will now review these outcomes one by one.

1 Change to less

What I learned from observing Syrian military checkpoints

My first job ever was as an external auditor at Deloitte. I was twenty-one years old and had just graduated from university. The job perfectly befitted its stereotype, especially for fresh graduates: I was epically overworked and underpaid. I still admire those who have the tenacity to endure a lifetime's career in auditing, yet at the same time I kind of feel sorry for them. I used to describe the experience as resembling 'military conscription': something that had to be done in a confined period of time, and that came with so much hardship, but at the same time instilled character and resolve. The job did have its merits, however, one of which was granting me the chance to travel across different cities in Syria and experience it as I had never done before. In a country that was so capital-city-centric, I found myself auditing the books and procedures of Chinese oil fields in the Syrian desert near the Iraqi border, a car dealership in the coastal city of Tartous and the largest detergent factory in Syria near Aleppo; and, of course, banks in Damascus.

I became more and more acquainted with the world of internal control, and learned about the 'best practices' that companies engage in to safeguard their assets and protect their businesses in so many different contexts. Never, however, would I have guessed that my outlook towards internal control would be influenced by this highly unlikely source: observations of the different patterns of Syrian military checkpoints.

At the end of 2012 my soon-to-be wife and I decided that we would settle in Beirut, in Lebanon, after getting married. Beirut lies approximately a 100-kilometre drive north-west of Damascus, with the road split almost evenly between Syria and Lebanon. Amidst the increasingly escalating war, we thought this arrangement would instil our marriage with a sense of normalcy in these chaotic times: dodging mortar bombs on weekdays in Syria, while spending the weekends in much safer Beirut. Historically it was always Beirut that was more dangerous, being susceptible to war, internal strife and bombardments, while Damascus was the safe haven. Amongst many other things, however, this had now changed. The century-old Damascus–Beirut highway links one of the closest pairs of capital cities (by land) in the world, alongside

Vienna and Bratislava, and Brazzaville and Kinshasa in the two Congos.

Back when my wife and I were still dating, I used to spend my weekends in Beirut and, right after dinner on the last day of the weekend, I would drive back home at night to Damascus, in a trip that I would make in one hour and forty-five minutes, including stopping at both the Syrian and Lebanese borders. This timeframe changed dramatically after the war developed, for so many different reasons. One main reason was the set-up of manned security checkpoints along the highway from the Syrian border all the way along the fifty or so kilometres to Damascus.

In early 2013, and following my marriage, the number of security checkpoints rose to six or seven from the border to Damascus. All cars would need to come to a halt and be searched. So many layers of internal control seemingly shielded the capital city and ensured that fortified checks were made against any possible harmful item that might make its way through. The number of checkpoints then rose to nine at one point. Even more robust, you would think? Well, not really. As I went back and forth every week, it was pretty easy for me to distinguish the effectiveness of control with the increased number of checkpoints: the more checkpoints there were, the more lax the checking became. The reality of the matter was that the increased number of checkpoints induced most of the soldiers manning them to rely on the search and frisking tasks carried out by the previous and/or subsequent checkpoint, which effectively meant that virtually none of the soldiers at the nine checkpoints really engaged in any thorough examination of our luggage and items. The soldier on the first checkpoint had a sense of assurance that if he was unable to find anything, the subsequent eight checkpoints would do so. The soldier at the final checkpoint felt that he had not much to do, as he believed that the car was searched thoroughly at the previous checkpoints. I realized that the greater the number of checkpoints, the easier it became for someone to potentially smuggle items in and out of Damascus, in addition to increasing tremendously the length of time it took to cross all the checkpoints.

The military eventually changed this arrangement, probably because they discovered the inefficiency of this multi-layered checkpoint system. The number of checkpoints was then reduced to just three, with one halfway on the road being manned by one of the most notorious army regiments, renowned for its discipline. The checks carried out by this checkpoint were extremely rigorous and thorough; a long queue would form, and each car would be checked inside-out, along with frisking through the pockets and personal handbags of all passengers. It was this checkpoint that became feared by all, as it developed a reputation for unmatched sternness. Having one main, robust control layer proved much more effective than increasing the number of checkpoints. I came to learn that, in change initiatives in internal control, sometimes less is more.

In the bank, and in light of the growing potential for fraudulent activities, our response was initially to increase the number of layers needed to validate the transactions done at the branches, such as deposits and withdrawals. We tested an initiative called the 'Triple Validation Project', whereby each transaction needed to be validated not just by one independent officer, but rather by three. Intuitively, it sounded like a great idea, as it theoretically aligned itself with the principle of independence and segregation of duties – the more people involved, the smaller the risk.

In practice, however, the result turned out to be similar to the ones I observed at the army checkpoints. When three people had to validate a certain transaction, all three became lax and counted on the others to make sure that validation was done correctly. Responsibility and accountability became diluted, and if a transaction was wrongly validated by all three, they could easily all blame each other. Though appearing robust in form, it was weak in substance and actually made it easier for fraud to take place. And it goes without saying that it also created bottlenecks and led to transactions taking much more time and to more queues forming, causing considerable frustration amongst both clients and staff.

So we developed a new approach, whereby we adopted a similar arrangement to what we had seen at the army checkpoints: one main validator was put in place, who became wholly responsible and accountable for any mistakes. We made sure that that group of validators had a reputation for strictness and discipline. Ultimately this led to decreased bottlenecks, a much more efficient validation process and enhanced control.

Having said that, we saw how increasingly difficult it became to choose the right people for the right job. One of the most visible consequences of war – apart from the physical destruction – is the moral decadence it can lead to. In a context as difficult and as conflict-ridden as war, people start increasingly to espouse a selfish and opportunist attitude in life. War can bring out the worst in those involved. I saw it happen pervasively around me in Syria. People whom we had otherwise always thought of as decent, law-abiding and ethical surprised us in war. A driver who had worked with the bank for more than ten years, and who had been renowned for being cordial and honest, turned out later to be heading a major robbery gang during the war, which ended up stealing some of the bank's cash during a routine cash transportation. No one would have ever imagined that this otherwise 'nice guy' would do this. At a competing bank, the three branch officers in charge of cash custody conspired, in the dying hours of the last day of the week, to steal most of the cash available at their flagship branch. This was discovered three days later, after the weekend, when the three officers had already left the country en route to somewhere in South America. These three people were also renowned for their upright behaviour and honesty. Many other instances have occurred, both in our bank and in others, where the harm originated from inside.

We learned the hard way that if there was a weakness or a gap in our internal control environment that allowed a potential fraudulent activity to take place, from either internal or external triggers, then in extremely adverse times that was bound to happen. It was only a matter of time.

In addition to carefully selecting the right people, the change that was needed was a revamping of internal control and the use of innovative techniques. Simply adding additional layers might be tempting; but, as we learned, it was not always effective and diluted accountability. Then you always have the problem of 'who will guard the guards'. There will always be a risk, if two or more insiders conspire. Diminishing this risk became even more important now.

Different perspective: how to find the 'ghost' worker

War forced us to be creative in finding practical, yet effective ways to revamp internal controls. We learned to apply a technique that is not an ordinarily classic textbook example of what can be done to revamp your internal control.

If you have doubts about the perceived riskiness of any issue, workflow or process, think of the harmless offshoots and peripherals of that issue. Write them down. A client of ours who ran a big factory with a couple of hundred workers started wondering if one of his plant managers in charge of recruitment was adding non-existent 'ghost' workers to the payroll and had developed a system whereby he would obtain IDs of his relatives or friends and sign for them as if they had worked, then cash in their salaries himself. As the number of workers was so high, it was very difficult to go down on the factory floor and physically look for them all. Even when our client tried to do so once and searched for them in person, his manager would come up with viable excuses. He would say that he had sent that particular member of staff out, or that he could not make it that day because mortar bombs had fallen on his route to work and he was forced home. Blaming everything on the war became very common, as it was an effective excuse that was hard to refute in many cases. Later that day the manager would call up his cousin and ask him to show up the next day, and would then introduce him to the factory owner.

We learned that changing to analytical methods that actually took less time to engage in were better suited to identifying such risks. We asked the client to prepare a concise list of the corollaries related to the recruitment of staff, as every staff member should have the following in their employee file: tax payment – social-security payment – number of days off taken – overtime hours worked, and so on.

We then analysed these items. Tax and social-security payments can be processed correctly even if the staff member is fictitious, in the sense that they do not physically attend work. These payments are mostly withheld internally by a company and paid directly to the authorities. Now we came to the number of days off taken. Every staff member should, in both practice and theory, take days off. If you run a report showing which staff did not take any days off during a period of one year, then this group of staff should be investigated. It is highly unlikely that someone would never take a day off for such a long time. If that staff member is fictitious, it is highly unlikely that the person who started this fraudulent transaction will have taken the time and effort to submit a day off for that fictitious person. *Voilà* – this is what we advised our client to do. A report was generated of those who had not taken a single day off in the past year, revealing that around thirty people had not taken any days off. Virtually all of them turned out to be fictitious staff.

In war, we learned more effectively the increasing importance of deterrence, innovative analytical methods and focused internal controls to revamp the safeguarding of our business.

In control environments across the world, businesses tend to be driven to add layers, complicate access controls and continuously add layers for validation. While some additional layers are necessary in many instances, we learned that sometimes less is more. One strong control point can be more effective than five mediocre ones. Complacency arises when the chain becomes longer and when accountability becomes diluted. And undertaking analytical tests when it is hard to scrutinize small operational risks proved very effective for us. They require some innovative and analytical thinking, and should at all times cover all those areas where you perceive increasing risk, and where conventional risk-mitigation techniques prove impractical, costly or difficult to apply, due to the circumstances. You will need to depend more and more on such analytical tests, which you will find can prove more effective than physical oversight at all times.

2 Change to more

Why it's okay to have ten different profit figures

Creative accounting is bad. Creative finance, however, is good. Having the right information at the right time is always vital; even more so during adverse times. This means that your financial planning and analysis need to be on a par with the changes around you, because many of the metrics, ratios and dashboards that you have been using prior to these adverse times will now be deemed less relevant.

Finance people are usually associated with being fixated on figures and ratios, and many take a myopic approach, in which the achievement of a particular ratio or target becomes an end in itself. The person in charge of your financial planning and analysis should be highly analytical, adept at dynamically understanding the changes around them and what this means for the analysis. Finance people love to act by the book, and in many cases rightly so, and what I am suggesting does not entail any deviation from standard ethical practices or a revolution in financial reasoning. Rather, I am advocating a dynamic approach to continuously adapt the financial tools and models to meet the changing environment.

Here one should not become fixated on not changing the 'unchangeables'. Unless they represent your crown jewels or key assets, many things that we view as unchangeable have been unnecessarily given this illusory and untouchable label. If transforming your financial analysis approach enables you to better analyse your position and assess how you stand vis-à-vis your competitiveness in fulfilling the CSFs, then this is something you should be doing more of, rather than being fixated on a self-imposed 'unchangeable' nature.

Let us take a very simple example. Let us assume that one US dollar (USD) equated to fifty Syrian pounds (SYP) on 1 March 2011. As a bank, you have deposits in several currencies, including USD, and you present your overall deposits by consolidating all of them in SYP and presenting them in this currency. This works in normal times, when only small fluctuations in exchange rates happen.

So let's assume that on 1 March 2011 you had 100 USD and 10,000 SYP as your total deposits. This would be presented on a consolidated basis as a total of 15,000 SYP. Turmoil hit and the market has become more volatile. The foreign exchange rate changes to USD 1 = SYP 100. Clients withdraw USD 50 and SYP 5,000, representing 50 per cent of your deposits. At the end of the month you end up with USD 50 and SYP 5,000; this adds up to a total of SYP 10,000 (using the new foreign exchange rate). Analysing the total balance of deposits would lead you to believe that this represents a 33.33 per cent drop. In fact your deposits have dropped at a higher rate of 50 per cent; the former ratio is being weighted by the depreciation of the Syrian pound.

Working in normal times does not usually expose finance people to such adverse changes in short periods, so it is likely they will miss what appear to be very noticeable structural changes. Your finance analyst should be able to quickly spot the effect of this currency depreciation and not allow it to mar the accuracy of the overall calculation of your drop in deposits.

The example given above is a very simplistic one of 'abnormal' changes that take place concerning many of the figures and ratios that you work with. So you will need to work with a lot of 'adjusted figures'. This requires both excellent analytical skills and flexibility in working around such adjustments, as well as acceptability by the decision-maker. Many finance people have good analytical skills, but become too obsessed with the manner in which calculations are made, so they are not always willing to exercise the flexibility required to adjust figures, even if that compromises the genuine accuracy of the figures or ratios in place; this obsession leads to dysfunctional behaviour in which the form overrides the substance. Here we can see the finance analyst refusing to adjust a formula to more accurately reflect a structural change in the underlying context, so as to preserve the integrity of this textbook calculation; the analyst does not realize that, by doing so, they in fact violated the integrity of what was essentially being analysed, and have thus presented what could very well be a misleading figure to the decision-maker. This is not what good financial analysts do.

I used to head the financial management and planning functions at the bank and had many different adjusted-net profit figures. I admit that on several occasions this caused a fair bit of confusion to the board of directors, but once I had provided the explanations behind all these changes, the dust would settle a few minutes later and most people would appreciate all the changes.

Below are some examples of changes that we incorporated into our calculations to highlight the typical areas where such adjustments were likely to be required when working in a crisis, to ensure a more accurate reflection of the state of our organization.

i) Operational vs non-operational item segregation

Income statements are usually divided between operating and non-operating sections, segregating the respective income and expense amounts on the basis of whether or not these were made/incurred as a result of the core everyday operations of the company. In normal situations, the non-operating results are not significant, and the distinction between the two is clearer. In adverse times, you will probably be subjected to more exceptional or *extraordinary* events, leading to an increased surge in non-operating items. You will probably have to take higher provisions, you could be subjected to theft or you could make extraordinarily high income from an unlikely source, and so on.

A lot of operational items will at the same time exhibit features that make them more *extraordinary*, therefore probably rendering them as non-operational.

For example, all banks usually have provisions for their doubtful debt; in healthy environments this usually ranges between 0 and 2 per cent of overall loans. This means that banks usually set aside funds assuming that between 0 and 2 per cent of their total loans will become bad loans (borrowers won't pay them back), and banks consider these as potential losses and expenses. Before the war, our ratio fell in that range, and this balance of provisions was always classified under operating expenses, because provisions are taken on loans that represent a core offering of a bank.

In war, this ratio shot up to around 40 per cent. Many might argue that the item remains operational, but this significant increase – coupled with the fact that there emerged a diminished control in decreasing this figure, due to the deterioration of the crisis – forced us to rethink the place of this item in the income statement. Continuing to show it under an operating expense item would mean that our operational profit would fall significantly, as this figure alone would greatly tilt our operating figure. We asked how relevant this figure was to the core individual operations of the bank? The increase in provisions represented a systematic occurrence that took place amongst the entire banking sector, and so letting this figure scar our operational profit analysis would skew and remove our focus from our core operating drivers, which we had more leverage to change and act upon.

As such, two important criteria emerge. The first is controllability: how able are you to control the drivers relating to that certain figure? The second refers to how systematic this figure has become – as in whether it applies solely to you or to the system as a whole. Compounding the effect of systematic factors that affect all other competitors in your calculations would greatly decrease the focus on your individual performance, and on what can actually be done to improve it. It becomes all too easy to become overwhelmed by worse trends and figures, and thus instead of confining the analysis and efforts to the areas that you can improve, you become inclined to blind yourself to them. I have seen this so many times and it is all too common. Truly analysing your operational and non-operational items, and making the right segregation in light of the above, is essential to accurately analyse your company and make the right recommendations. It's okay to have three or four adjusted figures for operating profit, each used in a separate context. Your board or CEO will get used to it, when you explain clearly the rationale behind them.

ii) Exercising care in assumptions

Budgeting plans, feasibility studies, valuation models and other plans that similarly entail a projection into the future require assumptions. Assumptions are more difficult to make in a time of crisis plagued with uncertainty.

Let's look at valuation, for example. Valuing companies requires in many methodologies a projection of future free cash or dividends. This entails the need for both a stable rate to discount these cashflows at, and figures from a past period to use as a basis to project future cashflows. In times of crisis, it might prove daunting to establish an accurate discount rate that projects into the future, especially if there is increased uncertainty on interest rates, as was the case in Syria with periods of hyperinflation.

What also complicates the matter is that using figures in past periods during normal times to project earnings is unlikely to be accurate, because past periods are not likely to be reflective of the underlying context of the future. Future valuations carried out using such factors will be very problematic. The financial analyst should be able instead to analyse rigorously the said factors and try and identify the areas of tangible and intangible value. Perhaps owning a certain real estate, capability or certain connections in the market will mean so much more in adverse situations than the effect of certain figures, which might prompt them to consider these as the main basis for valuation. It is important that the analyst exhibits this flair for analysis for identifying the true determinants of value that need to be measured. A more reflective basis for valuations could very well be identified and used that does not necessarily conform to a textbook basis, for after all the situations you are facing might be far from textbook circumstances and so a different approach is warranted.

Let's examine another type of study where we faced difficulties in making assumptions. We had to calculate the savings or expenses resulting from the closure of certain branches of the bank. When branches, offices and other physical retail channels usually close down around the world, this is most likely attributed to commercial reasons – and not because jihadists have stormed the city, as happened to us in a few cases. For many of our branches, it was a mix of security and commercial reasons that led us to either close them or consider closing them. Each branch had its own unique set of challenges that were evolving by the day. A branch could be doing well, but the security risk simply became too high, as in Raqqa, where we had no option but to close it just before jihadists stormed it, after which Raqqa became the self-declared capital of ISIS. For such a case the model to determine the financial effect of that closure was not a simple analysis of the expenses of that particular branch, where we could roughly assume that all or most of these expenses would be spared. It was far from being that straightforward. We had to ensure that we correctly quantified the effect of such closures, whose factors changed from branch to branch. For every cost item, we undertook an analysis of whether or not that certain expense would continue to be incurred after such a closure. For many of our branches, it was revealed that most expenses would actually not be spared, even if we closed them.

There were difficult questions that we had to answer. If we were paying rent for a branch in a city that had now been rampaged by jihadists – and which we were technically occupying, but obviously not using – should we renew our rent contract? As we actually kept these branches in the hope of reopening them in the future, and did not lay off the employees, but rather arranged for their transfer elsewhere, many expenses pertaining to salaries, depreciation and rent continued to be charged as before. For some branches we actually had to incur more expenses, such as the cost of relocating and rehousing some of our staff. As we had to service the clients of these branches from other branches, we had to incorporate also the expected incremental increase in expenses resulting from servicing these clients. Our Raqqa branch might have closed, but we still had bank accounts opened by people from Raqqa who had relocated to other cities and now needed servicing from there. The cost of serving these people had to be incorporated. Only when making all these reasonable adjustments were we able to calculate the net effect from closing such branches.

Such adjustments were critical to ensure that the figures we presented reflected the situation as it was, with all its difficulties. In such problematic circumstances, adjusting such assumptions when conducting feasibility studies is essential, in order to be able to identify and single out the exceptional effects that were profoundly distinctive.

Having a transformed financial analysis approach becomes fundamental in enabling you to dynamically change your assumptions, so that you are able to provide reliable and accurate information that is more reflective of the growing intricacies and unique challenges accompanying the adverse situations that you face.

3 Remain still

After careful deliberation, and following the decision-making process of identifying the need for change, sometimes the outcome will be to remain still. No change is needed.

An excellent leader in extremely adverse times is one who knows when to remain still and when to change. Such a leader knows that staying still is an active decision that does not equate to passively *not* making a change. This decision might stem from different reasons, as follows:

1. The system currently meets growing challenges in an optimal way. The crisis does not directly affect the way things are done. Changing things will hamper the way things are currently being done.
2. Resources are limited. This area is not a priority and is not directly aligned with the CSFs. It is better to focus resources on other areas instead.
3. Change might improve operational capabilities, but will jeopardize other more critical areas, such as affecting morale or unnecessarily tackling some deeply embedded organizational cultural values.
4. Change will entail toying around with the organization's crown jewels or core values, which is unnecessary.
5. The change being called for is aligned with individual goals and purposes that are not aligned with organizational goals.
6. Change is not driven by organizational necessity, but rather by individual staff comfort.
7. Change will unnecessarily shock an otherwise working system where the cons outweigh the benefits.

4 Remain passive; don't do anything

As challenges become more and more difficult, the worst thing you can do is evade the relevant ones by not assessing their implications. Whereas remaining still is an active process that comes after careful deliberation of all the options and has merit, remaining passive is not doing what is required to assess whether or not you need to change. By not changing when you need to, you are not adapting to the growing challenges and responding to them. By not responding to them, you are allowing your organization to become more and more vulnerable to the perils of the ongoing crisis, and are not allowing yourself to see the opportunities ahead of you.

5 Change things half-heartedly

Unfortunately this is a very common course of the action taken by many people, where a barrage of change decisions are taken, with little commitment on actually following them through. Sometimes the decision-making process is weak, in that decisions are taken to effect change, but because they are taken for the wrong reasons or due to flawed reasoning, the organization does not *really* have the commitment to follow through.

The basics are quite simple in this regard: if something needs to be done, then it needs to be done entirely. If it isn't, then it isn't supposed to be done.

The focus of this chapter has been on highlighting the importance of determining whether something needs to be changed, as this is where effective leadership is required in a crisis. When this is not done properly, a string of half-committed decisions are taken, where there is no buy-in and little follow-up. Resources are utilized, time is wasted and an incoherent route is taken to effect these changes. Such initiatives stress the system, don't get the commitment that is required and, most importantly, never get done. Half-hearted approaches also do damage in portraying your organizational leadership as indecisive, undisciplined, uncommitted and unable to do the things it wants to. It is a weakness that can be easily felt by both your staff and your competitors. No half-steps should be taken. Either take the full step, if necessary, or do not take the step at all, if it is not needed. If you stand on the edge of a cliff next to another, with a gap in the middle leading down to a valley, you should either take the leap to the other cliff or remain where you are. Take a half-leap and you drop to oblivion.

One area that most organizations jump at, early on in any crisis as part of their change processes, is cost-cutting. Cost control is essential, but the risk arises when it starts taking away an organization's capabilities. This takes us to the next chapter, but first here are some questions to ask yourself concerning change:

- How are you building the capability to assess the need for change?
- What inclinations in your context push you towards more change? Are there inclinations that push towards less change? Why is that? Are you aware of the merits and risks of each of these opposing camps?
- How easy is it to know whether the changes happening around you, and shaping your organization, are permanent or temporary? What happens if instead you rewire your mindset to align change actions with the evolving criticality of the CSFs?
- What are the organization's core values? How deeply embedded do you think they are? What positivity do they bring? Do you really want to change areas associated with them? How will people react? What are the pros and cons?
- When faced with change requests, are you really digging deep to determine the root cause? Are you asking the 'five whys'?
- When you end up not changing, is this the result of a decision to proactively remain still or as a result of passively not doing anything?
- Are you making any changes half-heartedly? If something needs to change, then shouldn't the change process be fully dedicated, with the right resources? What would be the anticipated result of half-committed changes?

7

Cut costs, but don't slash morale

The tempting nature of cost-cutting

When an organization faces a crisis that is likely to last for some time, increasing strategic, operational and tactical difficulties will probably lead to some extent of financial distress. In almost any crisis with the slightest hint of financial distress, the inclination to embark on a cost-cutting initiative will not take long to kick in. In difficult times there is an almost universal infatuation with cutting costs. We see organizations laying off employees in tough times, cutting down on benefits and starting to undertake all sorts of measures to reduce expenditure. Managers love to splash out phrases such as 'We need to trim the fat' and 'We must kill the dead wood'.

When done correctly, cost-cutting is important as it ensures that the organization is able to minimize its cost base, alleviate unnecessary financial burdens and become more optimally positioned in confronting the challenges ahead. However, cost-cutting can become problematic when it becomes an end in itself, wearing away your organization's capabilities and eroding its core values.

In very difficult situations you will come to the realization that the commitment and dedication of your staff will make the difference, in many instances. At such times the robustness of your policies and procedures, which govern your systems and how your employees interact, might not be enough to save the day. What *can* save the day is your people's dedication. If they are not motivated, however, you may very well witness the demise of your organization's ability to persevere in a crisis.

Managers are typically drawn to slashing costs – it is easy to do, it leads to an easily measurable outcome and is the more convenient route to fulfil budget profitability targets. Which is easier: increasing sales by 10 per cent in tough times or decreasing costs by 15 per cent? The latter is probably easier. When everything else in a crisis seems plagued with uncertainty, and at a time when it's difficult to assess the outcome of any decision, cost-cutting stands out as being a rare course of action that results in a clearly quantifiable outcome. Furthermore, the performance assessment and budget mechanisms in play in many corporations reinforce this kind of behaviour. We continuously operate in an environment where decisions need to fulfil the criteria of satisfying SMART targets: that is, target measures need to be **S**pecific, **M**easurable, **A**ttainable, **R**elevant and **T**ime-based. So if laying off Persons A and B after one month would save us US $4,000, this target becomes very SMART. Cutting the use of coffee and tea for your staff is also very SMART, as it could save $1,000 in a month. These two decisions are very SMART and very satisfactory, from this framework perspective, and are quite easy to pull off; in reality, however, they could well be very stupid. For every cost-cutting decision that you consider, don't get fixated on how it conforms to being 'SMART'; instead, assess how it affects your staff morale and your organizational core values.

We found that applying four principles in cost control during a crisis proved helpful. They are as follows:

1. Know your cost-appetite culture
2. Understand your cost drivers
3. Motivate your good staff; lay off your bad ones
4. Keep some leeway – don't operate at the bare minimum.

1 Know your cost-appetite culture

Effective cost-cutting is more of an art than a science. Each organization has a different culture when it comes to 'cost appetite', and you need to ensure that your actions are aligned with this culture.

Sometimes these are linked to an organization's core values, as addressed in Chapter 6, where I talked about the time a proposal was made to stop paying salaries in advance, which was later – thankfully – not put in place.

It is imperative that the person in charge of such an initiative is someone who knows the culture and the particular 'cost appetite' of your company. Just like people, some companies are frugal even in good times, and others are generous even in bad times. With time, these traits become entrenched in the company's culture and define it. Taking a decision to count the stationery of your staff, in a company whose culture is usually characterized as generous, will have a far more profound impact than counting it in one where similar measures were in place even in good times. I remember that in the first bank I interned in, back in my university days in Lebanon, I was shocked that some staff labelled their pens with their names. This reflected the cost culture of that particular bank, which differed greatly from the culture in other organizations. At BBSF, people would never think of labelling their pens with their names. You picked a pen when you needed one. That's always been the culture. We did not exercise prudent control on these matters. It was the conviction always that micromanaging such areas would never be helpful, and the benefit of trusting people and creating that transparent culture far outweighed the perceived cost saving of a few pens.

This defined our cost-appetite culture and shaped the way people acted. Being aware of these facets of our culture enabled us to know which areas to introduce cost reductions in, and where not to. It is important to ensure that your decisions do not vehemently disrupt your corporate culture. This is what led us to add chamomile tea and other drinks to our hot-beverage offerings, rather than reducing them.

When we added chamomile tea to our kitchen offerings

I was entrusted in 2012 with the difficult task of leading a cost-cutting initiative. It was the second year of the crisis, developments were escalating quite rapidly around the country and the currency was depreciating considerably. It was one of the toughest periods in the war for me, and for many people. A meeting was held to discuss areas where cost-cutting could be made. As we sipped our coffees in the meeting room, one of the items that we discussed was reducing the serving of coffee and tea to our staff.

Anyone who barely knows the Middle East is aware of how ingrained the culture of tea- and coffee-drinking is in our everyday lives. Even when you enter the house of a poor family, the first thing they do is offer you tea. Many foreign tourists in the Middle East are pleasantly surprised when they are offered a free glass of tea by shopkeepers. Tea and coffee are elementary in our culture, as they serve as the first signs of the inherent generosity and hospitality of the people – as the Japanese author mentioned in Chapter 1 found out, to his surprise. Just search for promotional tourist videos of Arab countries on YouTube: in one scene you are almost bound to find the image of a smiling Arab man wearing a fez and pouring sweet tea into a glass in Morocco; and wearing an Arab headscarf and pouring coffee into a small cup in Jordan. You would never find such images in ads for Denmark or Finland. To break up street fights on Levantine streets, middlemen would typically invite both sides for a cup of tea – this is how central coffee and tea are in our culture.

Stopping serving these drinks in order to save costs would have been disastrous. Yes, it could appeal to the SMART code of thinking, yet it is incredibly foolish and counterproductive. That decision could have saved the bank around US $2,000 a month, leading to a calculated figure of $24,000 a year. But what about the effect of the sapping in staff morale? Not only are they operating in difficult times and are being asked, in many instances, to stretch themselves beyond their prescribed job descriptions in order to counter difficulties at work, but you also want them to do it without drinking coffee or tea. The effect would have been devastating to morale and, in terms of productivity, commitment and dedication, would probably have cost us far more than $24,000.

We not only decided to maintain the serving of coffee and tea, but also added additional lines of hot drinks, such as chamomile tea, green mint tea, jasmine tea and the Damascene floral *zhourat* drink. Such minor decisions entailed a small incremental cost, but would have a gratifying impact on staff. Even small decisions that slightly enhance aspects related to people's strong values and elements of their culture can have a high impact. In very tough times we learned always to appeal to the elementary sensory needs of staff, especially those needs that are strongly associated with culture and values. People will respect you for that. They are aware that times are tough, and they will appreciate that not only did you *not* compromise on the basics, but you actually improved the offering for them. They will view you as being noble; and – as addressed in Chapter 1 – they will appreciate that you decided to do the right thing, rather than doing things right, because they know that cutting the cost of all these drinks would have been the latter. They will remember you for that.

Never save costs by compromising on your staff's sensory needs, or they will come to hate you. Do not get them cheap chairs to save costs, or you will have disgruntled people with backaches. Do not turn off half the lighting to save power costs, or adjust the temperature control to make the offices colder or warmer. If you decide to go cheap on the basics, don't expect people to take that extra leap for you when you need them to, in difficult times.

2 Understand your cost drivers

Your cost-reduction actions need not have an adverse effect on people – we found ways to reduce some costs with virtually no effect on the well-being of our staff and clients. After being mindful of your cost-appetite culture, now comes the time to quantify your cost base and understand it.

First, make a list of all your expenses. Categorize them into broader groups, but analyse each expense item uniquely, as they have unique cost drivers. Detailed analysis matters here. Understand that you might have to experiment with this, so allow the possibility for revision. Try to determine what drives each of these expenses. So, for example, if you have electricity expenses – what are the cost elements? Use of light bulbs? Water boilers? Air conditioning? Cash-counting machines? The extent to which they are turned on? Computers? List them all. Think of all the possible cost components and try to quantify their impact. Involve people on the ground who might have an insight that you might not have.

Add one more dimension to your analysis: differentiate between expenses that are contractual versus those that are non-contractual. Contractual expenses refer mostly to agreed-upon expenses over an extended period of time, such as rental agreements. These are more difficult to change, but still need to be assessed. Non-contractual expenses are in theory easier to inflict changes upon. Look at their breakdown. Do you have more contractual expenses, or is it the other way round? Decide whether, in the particulars of this crisis, you might be better off having fewer contractual expenses in order to have better flexibility, or whether it is actually better to keep these contractual expenses, which could serve other goals, such as securing certain arrangements or guaranteeing an uninterrupted flow of certain services or supplies.

This exercise will enable you to come up with a realistic expectation of what cost categories can be decreased. When it comes to analysing these costs in particular, don't get carried away by being fixated on doing *less* of something. Don't look at your printing expenses and simply decide to print less paper. Analyse the particulars and establish the components of whatever increases printing costs. Volume is just one factor, but there are others. We looked at our printing-supplies expenses and determined that it was an area we needed to work on. We then asked to look at the forms used by our clients, and we noticed how many of these pre-printed forms were unnecessarily coloured. We made the simple switch to black and white and saved a significant portion of the costs. We didn't have to print less in volume. Large savings were made by making a small decision, with virtually no impact on the clients or the staff.

On other occasions we decided to launch automation initiatives for some of our manual processes, such as automating the manner in which we processed inheritance payments to heirs. This led to a short-term increase in capital expenditure, but in the long run not only did it save on our costs, but it also resulted in more effective and streamlined operations, leading to faster and more accurate transactions and thus happier clients. And we realized at some point that the water boilers in our thirty-nine different premises were all turned on during the night; so we simply put mechanisms in place to automatically turn them off at night, which slightly increased our capital expenditure in the short term, but ended up saving a significant portion of our power costs a few months later.

As the local currency was losing its value, one area where we exerted effort to save costs was in effectively 'hoarding' items that were purchased in foreign currency. As a bank, we used many supplies that originated outside Syria, where the costs were largely dependent on the exchange rate. We did an inventory of all non-perishable items that could be bought way in advance, and which did not risk becoming obsolete or outdated, if not used immediately; this included ATM paper rolls, bank stationery and other IT-related items. We ended up buying quite a large inventory of these items to use over the next couple of years or so. It served an additional purpose, for besides saving costs by locking in a known price, it also mitigated the risk of supply by ensuring availability in increasing turbulent times. This ended up saving us considerable costs, as prices did indeed go up in the future.

3 Motivate your good staff; lay off your bad ones

One way in which we boosted staff morale was by increasing our investment in their training and development, even amidst our cost-cutting measures and increasingly distressed times. Trainers in Syria were leaving the country, and the mobility of our staff was becoming more and more restricted. It was becoming very difficult to deliver basic training to our staff. Some of them in cities such as Aleppo, which was under siege for some time, did not receive any training for a while.

But we wouldn't let a siege and a 'government vs rebel' show-down in Aleppo hamper our training objectives for our staff there. We decided to be the first company in Syria to implement world-class e-learning as an elementary training tool. It did not come cheap, but it ensured that everyone in our branches had access to world-class bank training tools. Our staff in Aleppo who were almost trapped in their city in 2013 had the same access to e-learning banking courses on credit-risk management and trade finance instruments as a fellow banker in Zurich did.

We also launched a company-wide online gaming competition, where teams would play in a simulated banking market as virtual banks, and had to make banking decisions to compete against each other. The winning team would get a small stock-option reward. I remember speaking on the phone to the Finnish CEO of that gaming company in Helsinki, discussing the implementation of the game, and when I said that I was calling from Syria, he froze for a second and probably thought I was making a tasteless joke. I wasn't, of course, and the game turned out to be a big hit. Many staff would voluntarily stay at work for late hours to play and win. 'Gamifying' training proved to be a major success for us. People are competitive in general, and when you leverage this to your advantage, by letting them compete against each other in a healthy environment, your staff will feel cherished and motivated.

Motivating staff in tough times is hard, but keep in mind that just as your staff will become more vulnerable and susceptible to negativity, they will also be increasingly receptive to positive decisions in tough times. When our staff saw us investing in Finnish gaming competitions and world-class e-learning courses, at a time when exposure to services coming from outside Syria was becoming more and more restricted, they felt far more motivated. If we found ways to instil motivation in people in a besieged city, then you are likely to find ways to motivate people anywhere.

Some people, however, cannot be motivated and have proven that they are bad eggs. Their negative impact has outweighed any positive value they might bring to you. They need to go.

Who to lay off? Ask the janitor

One major cost-cutting initiative is the lay-off of staff. In normal times organizations are sometimes capable of accommodating 'bad staff'. This term can be problematic, because it can refer to many different types of staff, depending on the industry, the organizational culture, the legal environment and the country. In some fast-paced industries, someone who doesn't achieve their target automatically becomes 'bad'. In others, someone with an attitude problem is 'bad'. In others still, someone who doesn't 'fit with the organizational culture' becomes 'bad', whereas underperformers are not always seen as bad staff. There are so many different interpretations, and it is beyond our scope to address them here. What concerns us is how, in a crisis, the added challenge of negative contagion arises, which can make 'bad staff' even 'badder', or can create a new group of 'bad staff' that is different from the first.

In a crisis, people become more vulnerable and susceptible to negative energy as stated earlier. As the context has become more troubled, it becomes far easier for people not only to pick out the negatives, but to amplify their impact and wreak havoc within. Although people's propensity for appreciating noble acts will heighten, as mentioned above, by the same token their immunity will deteriorate and they will become more easily swayed by negative forces around them. In a crisis with increasingly pressing

challenges, amid a distraught environment, it will become far easier for bad people to affect good people with their negative energy,
rather than the other way round. No matter how you define the
'bad staff' in your organization, in a crisis a group of people will
emerge with a negative attitude, who are unwilling to apply the
new principles that you are advocating; who are unproductive and
prone to stirring up negative emotions and demotivating people
around them. They are the staff who have proved themselves incapable of changing along the lines dictated by your strategic objectives
and operational tactics, in spite of several attempts to persuade them
to. These staff should be removed. There are legal requirements and
these differ greatly from country to country – whatever regulations
govern your actions, these people should be out.

You do not need to embark on company-wide analyses to identify these people; everyone knows who they are – even the janitor
does. You cannot hide bad staff, especially in a crisis. They make
themselves known. They should be laid off right at the outset, even
if it leads to some significant cost for you, if you have to offer them
a 'golden handshake' or some financial compensation to leave. It is
essential that you do this from the start, and quickly. These people
should not be accommodated within the organization, or you will
create a dysfunctional motivation system, as will be addressed in
the final chapter.

4 Keep some leeway: don't operate at the bare minimum

Cost-cutting initiatives sometimes remodel processes and operations in such a way that they are able to work using minimal
inputs. This does not work in a crisis. In Syria, all communication
lines were continuously going out of service, due to the escalation
of the war. Sometimes it was the landlines that were bombed. At
other times the mobile network stations went out of service for
many reasons. We had ATMs across the country that before the
war connected to our main servers, using one channel. In light of

these new changes in the environment, we had to ensure that the ATMs were working in an uninterrupted manner as far as possible. So we ensured that several layers of connection were established with these ATMs, using all possible means of communication. If the standard connecting lines were cut, the ATMs could reconnect using mobile technology, and so on. We set up different alternatives, assuming each stopped working. Such a set-up proved to be more costly, but it was needed. We were not driven by operating at the bare minimum, but rather by ensuring the continuity and sustainability of our operations.

As the crisis gradually escalated to a full-blown war across numerous fronts, we started having more and more staff fleeing the country. For the most part this represented an organic staff attrition, due to circumstances that we could not change. No motivation on our part would convince them to stay in the country and end up being conscripted into the military, only for them to find themselves fighting ISIS at the front line instead of counting cash at the bank tills. Because I had no brothers, I was exempted from serving in the army, according to Syrian law. Many others did not have this exemption.

During these times, when we had ten people doing the job just right in a certain department, with all the processes properly set up, we sometimes considered raising the number of staff to eleven, in anticipation of this attrition. We avoided the temptation to operate at minimal capacity. We did not get overwhelmed by the use of some productivity metrics and let them take precedence. This may work in a normal environment, but in a crisis you need to assess whether operating in the most efficient way possible could hamper your capability to be flexible, and your ability to respond to changes in the best possible way. Establishing this mode of thinking was very difficult at first. The urge to continuously make things more efficient, while utilizing the least amount of input, has become embedded within corporate mentality. Modern business practices have become more and more driven by the need to optimize and improve efficiency – and in many cases rightly so, but not necessarily in a crisis.

When you are managing in a crisis, your set-up should be redesigned in such a way as to respond effectively and dynamically to difficult changes around you. You will need to create buffer zones for your processes, arrangements and set-ups to be able to handle unexpected shocks. There will be some new principles that you will be applying – hopefully inspired by this book. You will be hit in many ways, and subjected to different shakes. The requirements of such a set-up differ from when you are operating in a normal environment, where you are able to become more efficient, with the changing input and process variables being known, for the most part.

Having said that, this is not a warrant to stop enhancing processes and workflows. There is a difference between what I call 'kinetic efficiency' – which should be enhanced at all times – and the efficiency notion, which, in its most radical manifestation, has engrossed workplace mentality with the zealous desire to ensure that everything operates at a bare minimum continuously. So back to the ATM example: kinetic efficiency ensures that the cash-withdrawal process runs smoothly and fast – here you have to be highly efficient. As to the efficiency of ensuring that you have just the right channel to ensure smooth withdrawals, then it is fine if you set up several alternatives to maximize the probability of ensuring the continuation of your services, no matter what happens.

Being mindful of the implications of keeping some leeway in your operations is important in a crisis, so that you do not get swept away in making decisions to work at a bare minimum in order to save costs, at a time when the need for a bigger fall-back cushion takes precedence.

This brings us to the next chapter, which talks about the importance of doing more and speaking less. First here are some questions to ask yourself as you assess the need for cost-cutting:

- What is your cost-appetite culture? What areas that might get affected by cost reduction are associated with your core values? What about the areas that relate to the

immediate sensory needs of your people? What do you
think will be the impact on people's motivation?

- Do you really understand your cost base and drivers?
- When analysing particular costs, are you focused just
  on spending less on something? What other criteria are
  there that can be assessed for potential cost-saving
  opportunities?
- Who are your 'bad staff'? How are they affecting the
  people around them? How does keeping them around
  affect overall organizational performance?
- In a crisis, how can you create more buffer zones to
  anticipate the growing likelihood of shocks? What is the
  risk of operating in a crisis at the bare minimum?

8

Do more and speak less

When our main founder abandoned us

As I sat in the office working late in the late autumn days of 2011, building models for next year's budget, as I usually did at this time of the year, I couldn't help but think how different things were exactly a year ago, before the troubles started. I reclined in my seat and took a deep breath, looking around the empty corridors of the bank just outside my office. Although the view inside the office had remained unchanged in the past year, outside the bank's walls an immense sea of changes had swept up the region and engulfed the country in a crisis that was only escalating.

It had been around eight months since the unrest first erupted, and a couple of months since we managed to emerge strongly from the run-on that occurred at the outset, when many of our clients flocked to withdraw their cash. In spite of all this chaotic commotion, mundane things like the annual budget still had to be prepared. But it was a whole different exercise this time round, having to build assumptions and create models based on them when almost everything was in question. I recalled some of the budget guidelines from our crisis-management committee, composed of board members and representatives from our founders, the Saudi Arabian bank and the Lebanese bank, in a conference call that had taken place a couple of days beforehand. These guidelines were aimed at making us more flexible in accommodating changes that were happening around us. I adjusted my seat back and returned to my spreadsheets, lighting up a cigarette. Yes, I was able to smoke indoors after hours inside the bank. It was one of the rare perks of working late when everyone else had gone back home.

My mum called then. I assumed she wanted to know when I was going to see her that evening.

'Louai *habibi* [my love], why didn't you tell me the Saudis have abandoned the bank?'

'What, Mum?'

'It's on TV! Banque Saudi Fransi just announced that they have withdrawn from the board of directors of their Syrian affiliate. This is why you you've been working late recently, right?'

I paused for a second. This couldn't be happening. My mother *must* have read something wrong. If this was ever going to happen, the last thing I would have imagined was finding out from my own mother. I knew those people. I had spoken to them on the phone just a couple of days before. A few months before that, I was in Riyadh discussing liquidity models with them.

I told her that I had to go, then quickly went to a prominent Saudi Arabian news website. My mum was right. The announcement was there in red, on their main newsreel. I read it again. And again. And again. I waited for a couple of minutes until it was played back again in the moving newsreel. It was no joke. Our biggest shareholder, who owned 27 per cent of the bank – whose representatives a couple of days ago were sharing their thoughts in the conference call on how we could be more resilient to unexpected changes – had just inflicted on us the most unexpected change ever. Our clients' reaction, in wanting to withdraw their money at the outset a few months ago, had led to operational challenges that were difficult to manage; but, as addressed in a previous chapter, we understood the rationale behind this systematic panic. Our clients' reaction was somehow expected. However, this action by our owners was unexpected.

A mix of feelings erupted inside me: a rare blend of disgust, betrayal, demotivation and sheer helplessness. If our main owners had given up and did not even have the decency to tell us, why was I sitting here doing what I was doing and having to motivate others to do the same? Even if they wanted to leave us, for perhaps politically related reasons, why didn't they at least tell us in one of their conference calls? Why leave us to find out from the news? Why should my mother know about this before I did? The Saudi bank knew exactly what this kind of news would unleash: fresh queues of people wanting to withdraw their own money. They knew this run-on would probably be even more difficult, whereby our reputation could be tarnished and people's trust in our ability to sustain our operations would be shaken. In the first run-on, the trigger was the onset of the crisis – a systematic event that affected everyone in the country and which we couldn't control. This, however, was not systematic; it was self-inflicted. Now everyone would see us as a broken house. Who wants to keep their money in a broken house? I wouldn't want to.

As I juggled all these thoughts I thought for a second that perhaps the CEO and the chairman knew, but just didn't tell me. I secretly hoped they did know and had a big elaborate plan that they had not told me about. Maybe I wasn't as senior as I thought I was, to be informed of such confidential decisions; but then again this seemed unusual, as I was always present at the highest level of discussions amongst board members. I rushed up to the CEO's room on the floor above. He was still in the office – standing and on the phone. He had relaxed his tie. He gave me a shocked look and nodded his head in disdain as he continued his phone conversation. I knew what his shocked face meant. Like me, he had just found out.

I retreated outside, waiting for him to finish his phone call. I felt that my world was crumbling. I looked down and saw two cleaners mopping the corridor. They were exchanging small talk and laughing. That's when I remembered the monumental challenge that we had ahead of us in reassuring our staff first, before our clients. We would open our doors to the public in around twelve hours' time. As I walked frantically back and forth, my mum called me again.

'Louai *habibi*, should I come with you to the bank tomorrow morning to withdraw our deposits?'

Turns out we had much less than twelve hours to start convincing our clients that the bank was here to stay.

As actions become harder, talk becomes cheaper

The next day I arrived at work an hour earlier than usual. A long queue was already forming outside the main entrance, and this time also near the staff door at the side.

'When are you closing?'

'Why didn't you tell us?'

'Do you still have money?'

Clients had plenty of questions, and rightly so. They were muttering different rumours about how we were going to close. Bank staff typically arrived fifteen minutes before opening time. We had exactly fifteen minutes to explain the situation to our staff, across almost thirty-nine branches in the country, who in turn had to explain it to our clients.

As our staff started coming in, most had blank faces. Many thought this was going to be their last day at work and that we were going to close. Those same people fearing for their jobs and their own financial security were, in a few minutes, to be entrusted with reassuring our clients that the bank was here to stay.

Following late-night calls with the chairman and some board members, our instructions were clear-cut. We had learned a very profound lesson a few months ago: actions speak louder than words – period. You can say what you want, but people will judge you by what you do. It is an almost universal belief amongst all cultures that action triumphs over words. In Arabic, we say that talking is the easiest thing in the world. In north-eastern Syria, the Kurds say that high mountains lie between doing and speaking. In English, it is said that talk is cheap. In a crisis, as action becomes harder, talk becomes even cheaper. Combining both the English and Arabic proverbs, talk becomes the easiest and cheapest thing to do in a crisis. It becomes the refuge of the bulls**tter, the incapable and the weak.

We told our staff that the bank was here to stay. We acknowledged that a partner had withdrawn from the board of directors of nine members, but there were seven remaining members with the strongly committed Lebanese bank. We made it clear that the members' resignation meant we needed to find two new board members to fill the now-vacant positions. This helped to emphasize that the Saudi partner was not indispensable. We kept the message brief – too much explanation and justification would have provided less clarity, rather than more. Ultimately we knew that it was our actions towards our staff and our clients that would genuinely reassure them, and so our actions needed to be clear and robust.

The least democratic countries in the world have the adjective 'Democratic' as part of their names: North Korea, Libya under Gaddafi, Laos, the Democratic Republic of the Congo and Algeria (whose president was forced to resign in April 2019 after protests swept the country). By calling themselves democratic, they don't fool anyone in the world into viewing them as being more democratic than, say, Norway or Sweden, although these two countries do not attach the word 'Democratic' to their names. Superfluous explanations and words do not add much value.

We decided to do almost the same as we had done during the liquidity crisis that we faced a few months before. The most effective way to handle this situation was to continue providing our services as optimally as possible. Clients wanting to withdraw their money? That was perfectly fine. Once again we showcased our banknotes in heaps by the windows. We sent out a short press release emphasizing that the resignation merely represented a change in the board of directors, with virtually no implications for our operations (which was in reality the case), and that we committed ourselves to working in Syria and to upholding our vision to become the number-one bank in Syria. But more importantly, we made sure that all our actions were aligned with this announcement. Anyone could write a reassuring press release. Living up to this reassurance was the more challenging task.

A great deal of noise and rumours escalated, both on social media and word-of-mouth, commenting vividly on how the bank would break apart, following the exit of our main shareholders. Some people attributed this exit to a political desire by Saudi Arabia to have the bank go bankrupt, so as to disrupt the financial-services sector in Syria. Others, who had little understanding of the legal implications of resigning from a board of directors, wrongfully claimed that the Syrian bank now had no choice but to close its doors and stop operations. Other outlandish claims stated that the Saudis actually took their money from the Syrian bank to Saudi Arabia, and had left the bank without any cash. Fictitious time-frames then started emerging out of nowhere. I had third cousins, whom I hadn't spoken to in ten years, call me out of the blue, asking me if it was true that they only had fifteen days to withdraw their money before the bank closed.

Whereas information can be technically defined as a set of facts or ideas, defining 'noise' in this context is more difficult. It can be a set of misinformation, misinformed opinions, rumours or an almost bastardized fusion of all the above. Noise continuously evolves and takes different forms and shapes. In some environments, where noise is inflammatory, it can travel faster than information. Twenty years ago only selected persons, organizations or entities had both the power and the means to disseminate information (and noise, for that matter).

Today, almost anyone has the means to disseminate noise using social media and, with the proper hashtags and influencers, can reach millions of people. With the recent ascendancy of 'fake news', the world faces a new information credibility threat that it has never seen before. Although anyone could create a rumour in the past, not everyone was able to broadcast it effectively. Today not only is this possible, but there is encouragement to broadcast continuously. With digitization, the capability of relaying information and noise has become empowered.

In crisis management, the principle is that relaying the right information at the right time is almost always recommended. When announcing a crisis, stating the company's perspective on it and how it will deal with it usually constitutes the first thing to do, to create coherence around the company's approach and communicate its commitment to resolving whatever is at hand.

In Syria, and given that we were operating in such a heightened hostile environment, we weren't facing a single crisis with clearcut implications. There was a myriad of crises that we had to deal with, covering tactical, operational, client-related and strategic aspects of the business. There was a lot of noise directed at us, and at our capability to serve our clients continuously. It will get noisy in a crisis, and it will always be tempting to spend time responding to this. It becomes tricky to handle, because the more you talk, the more questions emerge. Noise cannot be silenced. We learned that the right reaction was to dwarf its relevance by disseminating the simple fact that we were undertaking business as usual, in the aftermath of the exit of our Saudi Arabian partner. In tough times, people are consistently bombarded with noise, so they quickly become forgetful and find solace in actual facts and actions that they see in front of them. It only took a few days for our clients to almost magically forget about what had happened. As for our staff, we accelerated the budget process for the following year. You wouldn't do that if you were closing next week.

It will get noisy in a crisis – and no matter how noisy it gets, ultimately your actions will speak far louder than your words.

Even your name is not important

We managed to reassure our staff and clients that we were here to stay. Our actions conveyed that our main founder abandoning us had no effect on our clients' access to their money and on their banking. I still don't know to this day why the Saudi board members resigned. The most obvious explanation is that they did so because of political reasons, with relations between Syria and Saudi Arabia souring. But that still doesn't explain why they didn't at least inform us before the news was made public. The Saudi Arabian deputy managing director was actually a former chairman of our bank a couple of years earlier, and I reported directly to him at some point for almost a year. He was one of my favourite bosses ever. I have him on my friends list on Facebook and we occasionally exchange pleasantries. He cheerfully congratulated me when I announced that I would be publishing this book. Maybe one day I will ask him what happened back then. Or maybe I won't, because ultimately it didn't really matter. What mattered was that we responded effectively to our people's needs, and after a few days that was clearly established. Any other concerns or questions they had diminished in importance.

We wanted people to forget about the Saudi affiliate altogether, but it was hard to do so because of another challenge – one related to our own name. In addition to the rising challenges that we were facing across all fronts in the bank, the last thing we wanted to deal with now was an identity dilemma. The name of the bank was (and still is) a composite of the names of the two founding banks: 'Banque Bemo Saudi Fransi' – the last two words were the name of the resigning founder. The font used to write our name was the same one used for the Saudi Arabian name. If you do a Google search for both names and look at their logos, they are at first glance almost undistinguishable. Our own branding was so intertwined with our founder's that their abandonment of us posed what we thought at first was an identity problem.

We observed, however, that in reality people don't care what your name is, and we had overstated the significance of this 'identity' dilemma. Apart from a few instances when soldiers in Syrian military checkpoints cursed at the Saudi Arabian connection, when knowing where I worked, people didn't really care. But you could not fail to notice the irony of our press release, in which we said that we were not affected by the resignation of 'Banque Saudi Fransi' and signed off with our own name as 'Banque Bemo Saudi Fransi'. Names are sticky and we saw how, with time, reciting them becomes habitual, and the actual semantic implications or inferences become almost meaningless; they serve as a tool for labelling, distinguishing between different people and organizations. People form opinions on your identity based on your actions and not your words – not even those that are as central and dominant as your name. There was no need to exert effort in changing our name.

These days we see organizations exerting effort in changing the names of teams and departments. HR is slowly becoming an obsolete term – 'People team' is the new fad. I don't mind the changing of names, although I certainly would not want to see 'Finance' turn into 'Number-crunching team' in a few years' time. These new names might become more relevant as time progresses, but ultimately people will judge you based on the work done. People will respect you if you get things done, even if you have an obsolete or outdated name or designation – more so than if you have a more 'in' name or designation, but don't get things done. We learned that spending time on evolving our actions to meet people's changing needs, and responding effectively to the evolving crisis, was more important than making our name more relevant. Better to be called 'Banque Bemo Saudi Fransi' and have cash for our clients, than to be called 'The most independent and liquid Syrian bank' and not have any cash.

What sticks in people's minds is your actions and whether you get things done. In a crisis, when talk becomes cheap – and both the significance and the difficulty of action become overarching – this effect is magnified.

Never let your words confine you

During the next year or so, and as I personally struggled to get to grips with my own relationship with my city, Damascus – which I loved, such that even to this day I cannot recite its name more than three times without shivering a little – things took an unexpected turn. US President Obama blamed the Syrian government for an alleged chemical attack, and was to bomb Syria. A new dimension to the war had suddenly emerged, with US air strikes. I had seen US air strikes on CNN when I was a child, when the US bombed Iraq and Serbia. I had never imagined that I would one day be in a city that was about to be bombed by the US. But there was something new here: Obama said that he would first seek the approval of Congress.

By giving a timeline of his actions to everyone, the element of surprise – which I would think is elementary in any air strike – was gone. Lucky for us in Damascus, of course! When explaining the rationale behind the attack and other details, John Kerry, the Secretary of State, claimed that the strike itself would be 'unbelievably small'.

The way these American leaders restricted their threatening actions by their own words created a surge of unprecedented jokes amongst the people in Damascus, ridiculing the sheer stupidity of their comments. People would meet up to smoke a *shisha* while the votes of the US Congress (those who were for or against bombing Syria) were being counted. In one of many memes circulating that ridiculed Obama's indecisiveness, even when it came to bombing Damascus, one showed him saying that he wanted to seek the approval of the Syrian Congress before bombing Syria. My grandmother invited me for a big lunch before the hearing's date, to ensure that there was no chaos in the markets and that she would still be able to get good-quality aubergines for me, before the strike was to take place. Meanwhile there was heavy military movement across the city, with tanks and other weapons visibly and significantly moving around. Obama had unintentionally (though one might be tempted to argue cheekily that it was in fact intentional) given a grace period for the Syrian government to prepare itself for the air strike. A few days later, when the US Congress reached its decision, the Syrian military had had all the time in the world to take any measures it saw necessary to prepare itself for the strike. Thankfully, the bombing did not eventually take place.

What was striking for me in that short period of time was how, when the words of the leaders of the strongest nation in the world confined their own actions, even when they were bombing threats, it caused a reaction of ridicule and mockery. People respect assertiveness and decisiveness, even from their adversaries. Better not to speak at all than have your words be shaky, half-hearted and self-restrained.

When you allow your own words to unnecessarily confine your actions, you may be shooting yourself in the foot. If you want to do something, then do it. If you cannot speak about it without confining yourself, then do not speak about it. Speak about it when you want to do it. Do not restrict your own actions and take away the element of surprise, if that is important. In our case in Syria, I thank God that Syria did not get bombed by surprise, and that Kerry reassured us that the air strike was going to be 'unbelievably small'.

Be wary of unwarranted signalling and implicit commitment

Back to John Kerry – I had actually seen Kerry in person in a very unexpected place: dining with Syrian President Assad before the war, in my favourite restaurant in the old city of Damascus. Yes, they were friends before the war. I was dining there with my parents, and they were seated just a few metres in front of us. I still remember that Kerry was served *Kabab Karaz*, an iconic dish from Aleppo with succulent lamb meatballs swimming in a sea of deep-burgundy sour cherries. Whether he liked this particular dish or not, I couldn't tell. He did not give away any clear signals that night, when I looked at him. A few years later, however, he gave away clear, unexpected signals when he announced in 2015 that the US would take in several thousands of Syrian refugees over the next two years.

Taking in refugees is a noble thing. Being Syrian myself, and seeing my countrymen and women stranded across borders as they made their journeys in central Europe, sinking in boats on their perilous journey between Turkey and Greece and being humiliated in front of me by land border forces, from Hungary to neighbouring Lebanon, creates a dreadful feeling of helplessness and humiliation. But these feelings are nothing compared to the hardship experienced by those very people who had to flee their homes in the most difficult way possible.

What Kerry said in that instance was noble. But it carried within it a signal that few people recognized. By saying that this would happen over the next two years, he signalled that the war would take place for at least the next two years. There was an explicit commitment to the continuation of the conflict for that timescale. People do not want to become refugees. People want the conflict to end and to return home. What Kerry said resembled confirmation, from the leaders of the strongest nation in the world, that the conflict would not end soon; not for the next two years at least. The underlying message was perhaps not as clear to non-Syrians, but those feeling the heat understood it. What Kerry said was satisfying from a planning and logistical point of view, which responded well to the growing sentiment back then to welcome refugees. Little did he notice that in spite of that, he signalled a continuation of the conflict – either due to the US's commitment to prolonging the conflict or to their helplessness in being unable to do anything about it.

These two examples are rare instances in this book where I draw conclusions, based not on stories from the bank, but rather from the overall context in Syria. I was driven to highlight the impact that words have – more so than making any political comment on the situation. As I wrote this chapter, I almost felt it was wrong *not* to talk about the perspective in Damascus of the words of the biggest decision-makers in the world, which some readers might recall and may have perceived in a different manner. Being there on the ground, at the other end, meant that we felt the signals and confinement in a way that may not have been felt somewhere else. Although it helped us better prepare for an air strike, many couldn't not help ridiculing the words' shakiness and how they confined the speaker. The lesson was a very profound one for me.

Whoever was going to bomb Syria, at BBSF we still had to do what we needed to do, such as completing the budget. This takes us to the next chapter: Don't overplan. But first here are a few questions to ask yourself when you face a 'doing vs speaking' dilemma:

- Are your resources expended mostly on doing things or on explaining them?
- Are you delivering your messages through bold actions or merely through words?
- When you do speak, are you aware of the explicit signals and commitments you might unnecessarily be giving away?

9

Don't overplan

Let it snow

At the outset of the crisis, and in light of the escalating events in Syria, we quickly started working on developing our Business Continuity Plan (BCP): a multi-layered project that involved highlighting business processes across all operating cycles and categorizing them by several factors, including their criticality and the impact they had on different areas. So, for example, all transactions done by the finance department had to be assessed for criticality and for their financial, operational and reputational impact, amongst other factors. It was determined, for instance, that running certain reports for business heads was not critical – however, settling the payroll was. People needed to get paid even if jihadists were a few kilometres away. And so this task got precedence over other tasks and had to be done, no matter what the circumstances. A list was made of all the resources needed to settle the payroll: from people to desktop computers, from software to Internet availability and all the other elements that were required to ensure the payroll was settled on time.

In brief, the project defined the highly critical operating functions that needed to be undertaken in case of disruption, and itemized in detail all the resources required. Many large organizations around the world typically create such programmes to prepare themselves for when things go wrong in the workplace. The higher the stakes, or the greater the perceived risks, the more effort and resources are usually placed in such business continuity programmes. For us, the scale was epic, because the perceived disruptions were drastically different from those in organizations in other countries. In our case, the likely triggers that we perceived were extreme incidents, some as terrifying as ISIS taking over Damascus. Other possible triggers were a countrywide power shut-down, destruction of our servers and other war-related events.

We reviewed and identified every single activity that took place in the bank, and mapped it regarding its criticality and its impact on several areas. So, for example, ensuring the safeguarding of our customer data and updated bank records was considered highly critical, meaning that regardless of what happened, this needed to be undertaken, as it affected the going concern of the bank as a whole.

The design of the BCP required that all departments were involved – workshops were held and brainstorming sessions carried out to visualize what could possibly go wrong, and how we would adapt accordingly. This exercise led us to ask, for instance, where we would keep our backup disaster recovery centre, with all the servers and data. In case our main server broke down for any reason, this backup server would be used to restore all the bank's data and enable us to continue our operations. We had a few hundred thousand customer deposit accounts that were changing by the minute in real-time, with people depositing and withdrawing money across our branches. Imagine the disaster that would occur if the main server storing all this information got hit by a bomb and all this data was lost. How would we know our latest deposit balances? How would we know how much money people had in our bank?

Having more than one backup server was thus fundamental – but where would the servers be placed? Maybe in Aleppo? Ironically, Aleppo was one of the safest cities in Syria in the first year of the crisis, after which the situation there deteriorated so badly that its name became synonymous across the world with utter devastation. Or should one of the backups instead be in Tartous, the sleepy coastal Mediterranean town that was far less impacted by the war? Or maybe outside Syria altogether? There were regulatory challenges in play as well, governing all the little details, as the regulators made it clear that we could not set up any servers outside Syria. They did not explicitly say why, but I believe it was for reasons related to sovereignty, and to ensure that trust in Syria as a whole would not be shattered. If the regulators had allowed us to place these servers outside Syria, even if it was in neighbouring Lebanon, this might have signalled the message that they acknowledged distrust in the safety of the country. I assume this was the last thing they wanted to do, as regulators. They also did not allow the use of any telecommunication tools via satellite. Rebels were using satellite communication devices to ensure contact with each other, as these were far more difficult to intercept by the government. And so a blanket ban was placed on the use of such devices, and was very strictly enforced. It was therefore not an option for us. We had to rely on other means of ensuring uninterrupted communication.

What would be the triggers for activating one of the different courses of action prescribed in the business continuity programme? How would we inform the shortlisted team? Could we assume that there would be operating telecom and/or Internet infrastructures? Would there be operating electricity infrastructures, or would we need to generate our own? Would there be functional and safe roads leading to the space designated for working on these defined critical functions?

We came up with so many different scenarios, and tested this programme several times on different sites. We became more confident that we would be able to launch in preparation for any war-related event, to ensure that critical bank operations would go on, regardless of any developments in the Syrian war. We hoped we would not need to activate the programme, but one day we were forced to. The trigger for activating it was, however, something we absolutely did not see coming, and it had nothing to do with the war – it was a snowstorm.

It snowed like it had never snowed before in my lifetime in Damascus, blocking all the streets and halting all walks of life.

That particular winter day in 2014, fighting came to a complete halt for the first time in the Syrian war, with no casualties being recorded on any side.

Imagining scenarios in such a situation is incredibly easy; any-thing can happen, and no scenario can be viewed as absurd. When business continuity programmes are used in more 'normal' environments, these scenarios typically identify a limited number of known risks that affect a certain number of variables, where many other assumptions can be taken for granted. For example, a manufacturing plant in Japan with certain radioactive risks can embark on such a project, knowing that the main risks revolve around the effect of weather-related events or accidents that might take place inside the factory, leading to a possible leakage of harm-ful radioactive waste. The hazardous events triggering the waste can be visualized with much accuracy, although their probability and frequency may be more difficult to measure. Other general assumptions governing the macro context can, however, be taken for granted: an uprising in a neighbouring Japanese town, leading to clashes between rebels and the government, is extremely unlikely to be considered a possible threat.

In a war as horrendous as the one in Syria, virtually nothing could be taken for granted. There were imagined known risks, and unimagined unknown risks. This made the scenario-planning exercise daunting, and led to many excessive and unmanageable scenarios. Look at the map of Damascus on the next page – even if you don't know anything about the Syrian war, how tempting is it to imagine tens of different scenarios, with much variation in the internal and external context in play? Add in the fact that we did not only operate in Damascus, but in other cities, posing their own kinds of threats as well: how could we possibly prepare for hundreds of possible scenarios, each with their unique set of chal-lenges and requirements? We simply could not. No one could. And even if we could, it was impossible to plan and test and pre-pare ourselves for them. The project would have become too unnecessarily exhausting.

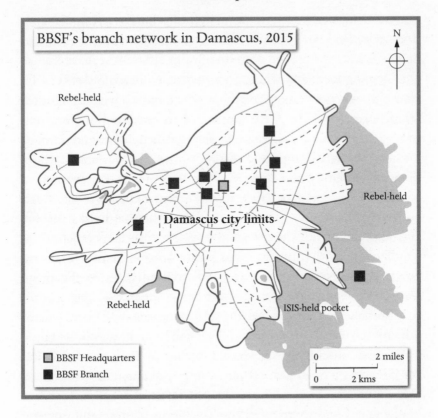

BBSF's branch network in Damascus, 2015

N

Rebel-held

Rebel-held

Damascus city limits

Rebel-held

ISIS-held pocket

☐ BBSF Headquarters
■ BBSF Branch

0   2 miles

0   2 kms

Conventional scenario-planning techniques entail condensing your proposed scenarios into a few scenarios based on the probability of certain events taking place. As this was difficult to measure, and due to the varying contexts that were imagined in our brainstorming sessions, we decided to come up with a condensed list of three scenarios, segregated by varying impacts and requirements in terms of staff, server availability, premises, cash and other assets. Three scenarios were manageable and could be tested thoroughly.

Referring again to the map of Damascus, you will see that we had eleven operating BBSF branches in the city, including our headquarters. Damascus was almost surrounded by rebel-held areas, with the ones on the eastern flank of the city ruled by groups armed to the teeth, typically launching mortar bombs indiscriminately on Damascus. Although the risk was perceived as stemming mostly from this side of the city, the war taught us that the risk could come from anywhere, and our branches were located across the city. Initially we were concerned with imagining different scenarios about who could attack, and when. So whereas in our early days of BCP planning we were more inclined to imagine specific scenarios taking place – where, for example, rebels entered Damascus and street battles flared up near our head office – later we started to focus on the actual impact instead. Let's say that we considered the likely risk might come from any one of four sides of the city, we would designate a branch to work from on the opposite side, staffed with people who lived in that area. Where people lived mattered, and we mapped all these locations along with the branches that would open. With time, the focus shifted less to visualizing the triggers of actual events taking place, and rather more to the effects that disruption would have. Rebels storming in – or snowstorms – meant that branches no longer became accessible and staff would find it difficult to reach their offices, and we had to prepare accordingly.

Without disclosing the actual scenarios that we used, let's consider an obvious first scenario: we would assume that eastern Damascus would no longer be accessible, and that both our branches located there would be unable to operate and our staff living there unable to come to work, whether they worked in branches or had head-office duties. To make things a little more difficult, let's also assume that our server was hit and there was no electricity and no Internet. With clear impacts and disruptions mapped out, it became easier to manage them. We planned according to the overriding impact, rather than spending the time visualizing the different possible triggers. We came up with a few different scenarios and tested them over several weekends.

The snowstorm that activated one of the courses of action entailed by our BCP froze many facets of life, including the banking sector in Syria. Remember that this is the Middle East and not a Canadian city; snowstorms on that scale rarely happen, and countries there are not typically prepared for them – let alone a war-battered country. We were so preoccupied with imagining extreme warlike scenarios that we missed imagining a more mundane trigger. Though this snowstorm did not lead to street battles near our head office, the disruptions it caused had many similarities to what a more warlike disruption would cause. A quick decision was made as to which mode to activate.

Although we had failed to anticipate this particular trigger, our response nevertheless worked. In times of crisis, it is likely to become more and more difficult to forecast all possible triggers, and any attempt to do so might be both overwhelming and futile. We found it far more effective to focus on assessing the *impact* of disruption – regardless of what caused it – on our critical activities and prepare ourselves for a few different scenarios, and to train our staff to be responsive and take the initiative, depending on the actual circumstances. It is easy to set your imagination free and get carried away with overplanning, envisioning tens of different scenarios. That is likely to overburden your time and resources, and might lead you to become so fixated on the triggers that you end up spending less time enhancing the resilience of the areas that will be impacted.

Scenario-planning, which was part of the BCP, was a very operational aspect, meant to ensure that we were able to continue working on the ground when disruption happened. It was not the only type of planning that we needed to do. We still had to continue doing the strategic and financial planning, which also posed their own challenges.

All is fair in love and war; except for planning

War or no war, it really was a no-brainer at the bank: budgets and plans still needed to be done.

The regularity of doing certain things at the workplace, regardless of whether we changed the manner of doing them, was not always straightforward to apply, when it came to our personal lives.

I had met the love of my life, Nadeen, in the early days of the conflict in Damascus, through my best friend and his family (thank
you, Bisher, Line and Sarah). She was Syrian, like me, and was also
British, owing to her father, who was a university professor in London in the late 1970s. We started a sort of a medium-distance
relationship. We lived in different countries, in theory – she was
finishing her studies at the American University of Beirut, while I
lived in Damascus. The proximity of these cities, and the ease of
travel before the war escalated, meant that we could spend most of
the weekends seeing each other, either in Beirut or Damascus. We
preferred Beirut, of course – more fun and fewer prying eyes. Fast-
forward several months later to 2012, just when the war was
becoming closer and more intimate, and in these increasingly turbulent and unsettling times I decided to do what people normally
do when they are most 'settled': I proposed. Nadeen, fortunately,
said yes.

Life had to go on – but with a lot more considerations. We started
questioning the plausibility of almost everything, including
whether we would have a wedding. How appropriate would it be to
have a wedding in these distressed times? When the big bombings
happened in Damascus in July 2012, my parents along with my two
sisters, one of whom has special needs, had to leave Syria abruptly
in the middle of Ramadan for Beirut, where I had to find them a
furnished apartment within a couple of days. My in-laws had to
relocate to Saudi Arabia. I had just secured a new living arrangement whereby I would be based in Beirut, but continue to work in
Damascus. Was it 'okay' to celebrate what should be the biggest
day of our lives? We were in the midst of war – so was that really a
cause for more celebration, to counter the otherwise-grim context,
or a cause for a less festive one, in line with the overall mood?

We then decided that we cannot be half-happy on our wedding
day. Throughout this book I make a recurring theme of not doing
things half-heartedly. It is one of those beliefs that grew within me,
and became more and more reinforced during the war, and which

I found relevant not only in the workplace, but also in my personal life. We saw other people who had half-weddings, thinking it would make them half-happy; I think it made most of them even more miserable than those who decided, out of principle, not to have a wedding.

Nadeen and I were going to get married and this was our big day. We had to enjoy this day for all it stood for. We decided to have a wedding – even if it meant that my parents would return that night to their small furnished apartment in Beirut, and that I would not be able to pick up my wife from her Damascus home with a traditional Damascene musical parade on our way to the wedding venue, as is traditionally done at Syrian weddings. Neither Nadeen nor I had ever imagined, in our younger years, that our wedding would take place in such a context, and in a different country. Regardless of these changes, we still wanted to relish our big day. We couldn't allow ourselves – in spite of all the hardships that we and our parents, and our countrywomen and men had to go through – to feel guilty for being happy.

So not only did I find myself planning a wedding in Beirut, a city where I knew little about all those people who offer wedding-related services, but I also continued to be involved in the planning of the bank in war. I lived in two parallel worlds 100 kilometres apart – possibly the furthest 100 kilometres between two capital cities in the world. I would meet florists in Beirut at weekends and hear about spring tulips, whereas on the weekdays in Damascus I would risk getting hit by mortar bombs on the way to budget meetings to hear about the reconfiguration of some of BBSF's networks. Looking back today, and as different as planning for a wedding and a bank in wartime were, I think similar principles applied. It is poetically said that all is fair in love and war but I do know from experience that it definitely does not apply to planning. Follow the temptations of fixating on numbers, stalling while planning, over-planning and inflexibility in changing your tactics – and unfortunate results could await.

Don't show me the numbers

The beauty of numbers lies in their uncanny definiteness. Numbers are exactly what they are. No implicit meanings and no vagueness. They are perfectly precise. Numbers do not talk back. Numbers can be changed, amended, reversed, subtracted, divided and multiplied. There is nothing surreal about numbers – the dilemma, however, is that despite their clearly quantifiable attribute, numbers can be very abstract. Anyone can throw in assumptions and insert figures, and draw out a forecast and a plan to go along with it. It will look real and specific – how it conforms to reality, however, is a different case.

In a crisis, when there is so much uncertainty, it becomes much more tempting to seek the haven of the definiteness of numbers. It becomes easy to get fixated on numbers, because when everything else seems so hard, numbers provide a source of sureness that few other things can. Numbers, in the form of budgets and forecasts, normally come together with any plan and form either the cornerstone of this plan or its conclusion. The conventional stereotypical image of a senior manager deciding on which plan to adopt is one where they are obsessed with the figures, single-mindedly skimming through the analysis and conclusions, while saying, 'Show me the numbers' or asking for the 'bottom line'. When planning in a crisis, I learned that you don't do it on the basis that the decision-maker at the end will start off by asking for the numbers, but rather by using a different approach. I propose the following model for planning in a crisis.

The Crisis Planning Model

You always need a plan, regardless of the context. Freewheeling into oblivion, and other outlandishly spontaneous actions with no active consideration of the overall direction and goals, does not work. It might work for some small start-ups, which have a unique niche that propels them at first, but at some point they will find the need to have done some sort of planning. There is much literature on the merits (and on the disadvantages) and the tools for planning. Here I am concerned with the model that works in a crisis, and which we have learned works best after a series of trials and errors. When I say 'planning', I refer to both corporate and financial planning, where the former usually revolves around operating plans serving to fulfil the strategic objectives of the organization, and the latter almost always entails the use of a budget.

1 Unswerving on the vision – flexible on the tactics

In Chapter 4 we addressed the importance of creating a strategy map (see page 57). At its heart are the vision and the strategic objective, which should rarely change. Tactics are then proposed on how to achieve these objectives, based on which you will probably develop your operating plans. Things don't go as expected, even in the most stable of environments. In a crisis, this is likely to happen more often than not. The overriding principle should be that you are unswerving and highly focused on your vision and your ultimate goal, but can show flexibility in amending your operating plans accordingly. The spirit of the plans should be focused on fulfilling the evolving Critical Success Factors (CSFs), which we have addressed earlier in several instances, which may entail that you change the way you do things in order to meet them. As such, changes to tactics don't become 'changes' in the sense that they become abnormal shifts to the way you are doing things, but rather they become the norm in this context, as normalcy becomes associated with habitually evolving your actions to fulfil your CSFs, as addressed in greater detail in Chapter 6. Changes to plans in normal times are viewed as abrupt or exceptional events. The mindset becomes different in a crisis. What is normal now is to change your tactics and be flexible in them, to meet the mostly constant vision. Tactics and operations are influenced by developments on the ground, and by tangible triggers and elements that will change in a crisis.

Before the war we used complex statistical financial models at BBSF to forecast the evolution of our customer deposits. This was a tactic or a tool used when there were operating plans in place to govern it. When the crisis started, these models became almost obsolete. Our strategic objective was to ensure optimal liquidity, which entailed the use of tools that were as accurate as possible to aid us in the analysis. It was perfectly fine to change the tool we used, as it no longer became relevant. Changing an operating plan is not only fine, but necessary to meet the evolving context. The worst thing you can do is let your operating plans be rigid and end up confining you.

2 Let your growing organic resilience steer you

By applying the principles outlined in this book so far, your resilience will have grown organically within you and your organization, and almost unknowingly they will be very helpful in guiding your planning actions. I will recall here some of the learning points of past chapters, and how they could revamp your planning ability:

- **Focus on the long term** – by playing the long game you don't let year-end targets override the vision, and you become more focused on building long-term capability to fulfil your vision. Your budgets and forecast won't be reduced to users asking first about the 'numbers', but focus rather on the long-term effect of your actions on your organization.
- **Shock your systems** – in order to become more and more comfortable dealing with uncertainty. You will become more adept at reacting fast, and at being able to change the way things are done, when necessary. This growing skill will enable you to become better at changing plans, when things on the ground take an unanticipated turn. Being accustomed to shocks makes you much more competent at dealing with things that have not been anticipated.

- **Be open to creating a strategic rift** – you should be open
to opportunities and understand that a crisis might be the
ideal time to create a strategic rift. So you should pursue
opportunities relentlessly when they emerge, and not let
any plans confine you. You shouldn't *not* pursue an opportunity because 'it is not in the budget' or 'not part of our
plan'. If you overplan, you might unnecessarily set so
many restraints and obstacles that you do not allow
yourself the space to be free to act, when required. A plan
should never impede you from grabbing opportunities,
and the process of planning should never be a dwelling
exercise that stretches for too long.
- **Become better at assessing change** – as this skill
improves, you will become organically better at assessing
the need for plans to be adjusted or removed altogether.
- **Situational leadership approach** – the more you apply
situational-leadership principles, as presented in Chapter 5,
the more organically equipped you will become to
change, depending on the situation. You become closer to
the ground, while still being guided by the overriding
vision.
- **Have backups** – this is important, as already discussed,
even if it means that you have to bear an additional cost.
Having buffers, safety nets and alternative channels or
means of doing things ensures that you can quickly
amend the way you act, with minimal disruption and
more efficient transitions.

3 Don't overdo it

It becomes very tempting to get carried away in a spree of overplanning – visualizing dozens of different scenarios involving
different disruptions – and the development of many different
plans. This requires a lot of energy, and the more planning you do,

the more pressure you put on yourself during the course of business, in mentally trying to fit what is happening today into the scenario you have identified. I remember this happening to me in the early days of the crisis, when I thought it was better to over-plan. I later realized that because we spent so much time imagining ten different scenarios, I unconsciously felt that the scenario we were going through in reality simply *had to* conform with at least one of the scenarios we had developed. This meant that I would abruptly affix all the forecasted elements and traits of that scenario to what we were going through, even if really that was not the case.

This almost forced transposition from scenario-planning assumptions to reality was so wrong because it created an illusory understanding of what was going on. I learned that overplanning might confine your course of actions, and prevent you from being liberated at a time when you need to feel unshackled by any hindrances to pursue the opportunities that might arise or to meet the challenges that lie ahead. As triggers become much harder to assess, the focus should instead be on assessing different impacts that might take place across your organization.

This leads us to the last lesson of this book. You can focus on the long term all you wish, along with focusing on all the other principles mentioned in this book – but if you don't ensure that the motivations of the people who are going to execute these principles are aligned with your goals, then the changes you wish to apply might not take place after all. Alignment, and never becoming lax, are essential and this takes us to the final chapter.

Before that, here are some questions to ask yourself when you are in the planning process in a crisis:

- Do I need to have a BCP (Business Continuity Plan) in order to plan for disruptions? What is the worst that could happen, if I develop a BCP but don't end up using it? What is the worst that could happen if I *don't* develop a BCP and disruption occurs?

- Is my scenario-planning derived from visualized triggers or from analysing impacts? How difficult is it to predict and plan for all possible triggers? Am I better off focusing instead on impacts?
- How flexible am I today to changing my operating plans to meet new challenges or opportunities? Do my current plans enable me to do so, or actually hinder me from doing so?

10

Align motivation and never become lax

Never become lax

I lived in Lebanon for several years. One thing that stands out in the country is the chaotic lawlessness, as displayed in many scenes of life – the most visible one being driving. Syrians would joke that even amidst the height of their war, Damascus still had better traffic control and overall road discipline than Beirut.

I remember in the early 2000s when the first traffic lights after the Lebanese civil war were installed, I would be ridiculed for stopping at the red stop-light, sometimes by police officers themselves. Even today, a red light means you are expected to stop, but it is considered acceptable that you drive over it, if you clearly do not see any cars coming the other way. In some instances you will feel forced to, as the cars behind you start to honk, pressurizing you to make a move. Driving in Beirut is absolute mayhem. Can this observation lead us to draw the conclusion that Lebanese drivers do not abide by the proper rules? Well, yes and no. What is astounding is that many of these same expatriate Lebanese drivers, who spend their summers in Beirut driving with low regard for the law, switch completely when they return to the cities they live in, such as Dubai. I have Lebanese friends who drive in Dubai, where the traffic rules are strictly applied, and they adhere to the laws as much as any other driver in the small Gulf emirate. The behaviour of that Lebanese driver therefore does not solely stem from their own intrinsic inclinations or characteristics. It would be incorrect to conclude, from observations in Beirut, that 'Lebanese drivers generally have low regard for traffic laws.' A more accurate conclusion would be that 'Lebanese drivers *in Beirut* generally have low regard for traffic laws.' The context matters. Here it is the overriding laws, and how well enforced they are, that motivate the behaviour of people to drive in a certain way. Similarly in an organization, the overall motivation system can crucially alter the behaviour of a person.

When working in a crisis, it becomes very tempting to become more and more lax. Complications will arise in the workplace, encompassing matters related to staff, customers and processes. Your staff might face challenges in reaching the office, in dealing with customers, in working properly with disrupting systems, in meeting deadlines and in many other aspects of their work. These challenges could indeed be genuinely difficult. Your staff will definitely require motivation in order to be able to cope with this increasingly difficult work environment. Leaders might be tempted to cave in to their immediate inclination to become more lax concerning the rules. Some staff might arrive twenty minutes after the working hours begin, and will rightfully complain about the chaotic traffic. You will gradually be tempted to start accepting many of their excuses. Your staff will ask for deadlines to be extended, or for certain work requirements to be put on hold. It will be challenging for you, because many of their requests will seem justifiable and reasonable in this context.

You will need to respond proactively to these increasing challenges; and the difficulty lies in being open-minded, understanding and receptive to the sincere difficulties faced, yet at the same time not becoming lax. Assessing the relevance of existing rules becomes key – if these are no longer relevant, then change the rules or eliminate them. Keeping them and becoming lax is the easy way out, in order to motivate your staff – or so you might think. Pushing the working hours thirty minutes ahead, even if that does not suit the organizational requirements, is an easy pseudo-solution. A month later you will probably notice, however, that many of your staff will start being tardy, even with the new working hours. Being lax never helps to reinforce adherence to the laws and create a more effective system – just as in the case of the traffic lights in Beirut, where being lax leads to chaotic traffic, and not more disciplined traffic. This basic principle fails to dawn on many people.

When convincing one of our Lebanese suppliers to visit Damascus during the war, he accepted the suggestion only if he was to travel with me from Beirut to Damascus, as he would feel safer. Thankfully, the two days he spent in Damascus were particularly calm. It was a while since I last met an outsider in Damascus, and I was curious to get his view on what struck him most about the city amidst the war. When I asked him, he gave me an unexpected reply. He was absolutely stunned by the fact that he saw government workers removing old flowers and planting new ones in the main Umayyad Square of Damascus. This particular display of normalcy amidst a devastating war was almost too surreal for him, and struck him most forcibly.

Affairs were definitely anything but normal in Damascus back then. But no matter how tough times get, you should not allow increasing chaos to permit you to accept a more lax environment. Engaging in acts that instil an air of normalcy – even if superficially so sometimes – is important to promote your commitment to orderliness and adherence to the rules. Enforcement of policies and procedures in difficult times is even more important than during normal times, as you do not want people to get accustomed to cutting corners and making exceptions, because once they do, a snowball-effect emerges, whereby many of your policies and procedures fall out of place, and breaking rules can become the norm.

In Syria we learned how war brought immense challenges, whereby a realignment of many work processes needed to be done to accommodate greater flexibility, but we also discovered early on that the solution was never to become lax. People will blame things on being triggered by the adverse environment. You need to ensure that you have the right judgement to accept such excuses, when warranted, and to refute them when they are not. Human behaviour is easily adaptive to expanding comfort zones, and it would be dire for people to have to readjust the other way round later on, when you start tightening up. As tempting as it is, never become lax.

Never budge to pressure

A crisis stretches both people and organizations. It reveals weaknesses and vulnerabilities. How you react, when you enter a confrontation, imparts a signal to people about the extent to which you will budge to pressure. If you do budge to pressure and there exist opportunities for these people – whether clients, employees, suppliers or other stakeholders – to put pressure on you to fulfil their own goals, then it is only a matter of time before they do so. Their motivation will have been shaped by your actions.

Some people will even be tempted to lunge at you, like a pack of preying wolves, the moment they sense weakness. We faced a few difficult employees at the start of the crisis, who were causing us much harm. We made the mistake of accommodating them. We kept them and tried to minimize their impact on operations. We thought that the only cost would be their salaries, which we felt was an acceptable cost to incur to avoid unnecessary confrontations. We later realized this was a big mistake. By doing this, we had signalled that we rewarded rogue people by giving them less work and by accommodating their requests. If we had started off with five people doing that, then we ended up with twenty people motivated to do that. 'Accommodating' these bad employees was not only costly, but also had a negative contagious effect on otherwise-good employees. Unfortunately, contagion spreads more effectively from bad to good than the other way round. Keeping the bad staff, without really needing them, was also doing things half-heartedly, which again, as I emphasized before, should not be done. If you want someone, keep them. If you're sure you don't want them, then let them go. It was us who were to blame. We had created a dysfunctional environment that signalled that we rewarded bad behaviour – if you slack and start becoming negative, then we will not only accommodate you and keep you, but will also decrease your workload and make it less stressful for you at work. If we could not get the basics right here, how could we expect to face the increasingly colossal challenges and apply many of the principles outlined so far in this book, as the crisis was gradually unfolding?

Luckily, we resolved this issue quite swiftly. Some of the people whom we wanted out were threatening us with dubious claims through legal action, and were asking for an irrational sum of money to stay put. What we did differently this time was that we established the endgame dynamics right from the start. In such a showdown between a renegade employee and us, we had the advantage of representing a corporation. We represented a legal entity, and any damages sustained would be on that entity, whereas our employee-turned-adversary was weaker, in that any damages inflicted would be on a personal scale. As such, by default we recognized that we were in a better position – the longevity or prolongation of any conflict was to our benefit, not the employee's. Our organization could handle dealing with a lawsuit for five years; they could not, as they most likely could not afford to wait such a long time.

We knew that most of these people wanted to get out of the country as soon as possible, so they tried to extract maliciously as much money through intimidation as they could. Even if they could wait, they would not want to. It was wartime and the currency was losing its value, so it was far preferable to expedite any potential gains. Most organizations in such a situation make the mistake of letting their adversaries sense that they want to get the case over with as soon as possible, which is what we – incorrectly – did at the start. All this did was empower these people, and led us to incur higher costs. Your rival hopes that you will try to get the case over with as soon as possible, so that they get what they want. We showed them now that we were more than willing and happy to wait and have the lawsuits stretch on in time – and they knew deep within them that we could. It was better to have these bad people out of the organization, and have a lawsuit stretching in time, than have them stay and spread negative energy within the bank. We knew that even if we projected higher costs in prolonging such cases, adopting this approach was essential to uphold the image that we were not easy to battle against, and that we did not cave in under pressure. It was amazing how, after we decided to use this new approach, all these unwanted people left within a few days and without resorting to legal means.

By showing ruthlessness in tough times and being fully prepared to confront the challenges ahead, you can thwart such attempts and, more importantly, create a deterrent for future possible cases. Your business principles and values drive you to act justly towards all your stakeholders, with the ultimate aim of maximizing value for them. Being ruthless in defending yourself, and using persistent tactics, is not unethical, provided you use ethical tools; on the contrary, leaving yourself vulnerable to attacks will ultimately affect the wealth of your shareholders and create a dysfunctional motivation in your organization, which could affect your operations and could thus constitute unethical behaviour.

Always align your goals, in good times and bad

Regardless of what organizational objectives you have, and which principles mentioned so far in this book you wish (or don't wish) to apply, people will ultimately be motivated by the drivers that govern their performance management on the ground – in other words, they will do whatever maximizes their individual return.

If you set a corporate objective that aims to increase the market share of your product/service, but your staff remuneration and/or assessment is linked to an increase in the market value of the share price of your company, you can rest assured that your managers will be driven to engage in actions that maximize the market value of the shares, regardless of whether that achieves your corporate objective. It is as simple as that – whether you are working in a Syrian bank in war-ridden Aleppo or in a serene Norwegian town overlooking the fjords.

We so often see dysfunctional behaviour that comes as a result of not aligning corporate goals with the individual goals of managers. Alignment is essential to ensure effective implementation of your strategic objectives. No matter how good your strategy looks on paper, if your performance management system does not effectively motivate people to achieve those goals, then you are unlikely to do so. You cannot rely solely on people's rationality and goodwill to achieve those goals. This would be wishful thinking, even when working in the best of times.

The importance of goal alignment is even more vital in adverse times. Working in such times means that your organization will go through increasing difficulties. Contexts will change. Some targets could be rendered unachievable. Any forecasting and financial planning process that requires foresight may be a complex endeavour, as it requires setting assumptions with increasingly volatile factors. All these are genuine concerns and do render the planning process a painstaking affair, as we saw in the previous chapter. People might find this state of matters a perfect excuse to act sluggishly and to blame factors outside their control. If they are unable to achieve a certain target, the blame will be attributed to a particular market trend or unexpected event that has been triggered. If they are unable to complete a project on time, they will claim the reason is an event outside their control. I have seen this set of behaviour be repeated so many times that it becomes a self-fulfilling prophecy on almost all occasions.

The easiest thing to do at all times, when things go wrong, is to blame external factors beyond your control; in our case, the Syrian war provided the perfect backdrop for that. It became increasingly frustrating at the outset to notice how many of our staff started adopting a more risk-averse approach, in areas where the overriding strategy clearly entailed a more risk-taking approach. We found that many of them wanted to stick to the status quo. They would ask, 'Why change anything or do something bold? Circumstances are difficult, and the risks are high.' The war became the ideal excuse – the perfect 'card' – that was tempting for anyone to use, from junior staff explaining why they were arriving late, to more senior staff justifying why they could not achieve their targets.

Some business practices advise the development of Key Performance Indicators (KPIs) as part of a company-wide performance management system. The setting of KPIs associated with the maximization of the long-term value of a company has become more common, such as tying remuneration to a long-term appreciation of the share price. Stock options have become more and more common, due to the conviction that they represent good motivators for senior managers to engage in actions that enrich the value of the company in the long run. Applying this in our case, however, was very problematic.

Our bank was listed on the Damascus Stock Exchange and, throughout the period of the war, the stock market has remained active. However, the dynamics of the stock market had little to do with the individual performance of companies. The war triggered many changes in numerous facets of the macro aspect of the economy, affecting currency valuation, the demand for cash and overall investment appetite.

As such, the stock market became less and less subject to organic market forces that usually govern the change in share prices. The announcements of profits, and the results of banks, would have very little effect on their share price. Therefore the share price could never have worked as a fair metric for performance management for banks. The prominence and impact of broad external factors, such as currency valuation and investment appetite, became more and more profound, so that it was only a matter of time until their effect on influencing the stock-market prices of listed companies started to gain more significance vis-à-vis the company-specific standard factors. Our revenues, expenses, profit and market share were so directly influenced by an increasingly diverse array of factors that it became more difficult to pinpoint the drivers of what caused what.

As mentioned in Chapter 7, we engaged in significant cost reductions. Our overall nominal expenses increased, however. A normal KPI analysis would conclude that the cost-reduction efforts failed. This is because such a normal analysis does not assume the possibility of a 50 per cent currency depreciation, which very well could happen – and did happen – in Syria within a short period of time. If your cost initiatives reduce the purchasing of a certain item by 20 per cent, but this item goes up in price by 50 per cent, then you will have an increase in expenses of 20 per cent. This overshadows the fact that your actions led to an overall decrease in the organic expense, as the reality is that the overall increase is attributed to an external factor beyond your control. The difficulty arises here in not only setting fair KPIs and metrics, but also in revising them upon assessment, to ensure impartiality based on the change of the prevailing dynamics.

It became very tempting to unleash a plan with tens, if not hundreds, of KPIs – again, similar to the temptations that we initially had with overplanning. This fascination with quantifying and measuring everything will amplify during a crisis, as the increasing uncertainty unleashes a yearning to have things be more certain and more measurable. Measuring things brings comfort and clearness at a time of little clarity. Knowing that a certain metric measures 88 per cent enables us to more confidently assess its success. Resisting this drive to make the performance management system easier and more comforting is essential. The worst thing you can do to your strategy is to put in place measurements that trigger dysfunctional behaviour to satisfy metrics with changing constituents. The exercise may very well be satisfactory from a quantitative point of view, but it will not only miss the whole point, but will hurt you. It will lead your people to have tunnel vision, whereby they are motivated to take certain steps regardless of what happens around them, to ensure that they succeed in achieving that metric, no matter how irrelevant it becomes, due to the changing underlying forces.

I have seen the above happen so many times, and what is most frustrating is when dysfunctional behaviour becomes the norm, driven by the company's own performance system.

Enhance your bulls**t-detecting capability

What needs to be done is to come to the conviction at the outset that working in a crisis requires a different approach. So many events that lie beyond your control will happen, as discussed throughout this book. Many metrics and ratios that work in 'standard' environments, where their underlying assumptions are fairly consistent, will become less relevant now, due to the emergence of anomalies. It will therefore prove difficult always to assign SMART objectives – **S**pecific, **M**easurable, **A**ttainable, **R**elevant and **T**ime-based ones – for many metrics. Many areas will be difficult to measure, but that does not mean that they cannot be managed. Most things can be easily measured superficially, and thus enable you to manage superficially, which will give you a false sense of being in control. However, the most important things will be very difficult to measure using a clear-cut formula, and will thus require an analytical corroborative approach to determine what had happened.

Your staff should know that you are not fixated on assessing metrics at their face value, and that you will pursue a more analytical approach to discover the root problems of every aspect related to the strategic objective. This will motivate them to act for the best benefit of the company, and to align their own goals with the corporate goals.

The successful implementation of this approach requires very effective communication of your strategic objectives. They must be understood by the key staff members. A handful of KPIs or metrics should be developed and the rationale explained, with substance presiding over form. It should be explained that assessment will not be done solely by looking at the figures, but will be further dissected to really identify the causal effect. Achievement of a good ratio could very well be the effect of a factor beyond the control of a manager; in which case many people will remain silent about it, in order to get the credit. If it was the other way round, it would be the first reason to be highlighted. This is part of human nature; it explains how many of us behave. But when the goals are explained clearly, and it becomes apparent that assessment will be made based on an intrinsic analysis of the underlying circumstances and dynamics, then people's behaviour is inclined to be different.

We once implemented a bonus scheme for collecting bad debts, where those staff who collected more debt would get paid a higher bonus. In a certain month we noted how one staff member collected so much debt that it seemed unreasonable. Further analysis revealed that the bonus model we had put in place created a loophole whereby someone could artificially increase bad debt and then collect it, thereby increasing their collection and thus their bonus. If you have a performance management system in place with such gaps, it is only a matter of time until it becomes abused. You might, rightly, believe in the integrity of your staff, but bear in mind that motivation is also a very strong driving force. Such performance systems should be very articulately designed and tested.

Having a few KPIs that relate to the strategic objectives mentioned in the strategy map (see page 57) ensures a focus on what matters most. Operating plans must be developed for each department, highlighting the tactics to be adopted, though these can be flexible, according to prevailing conditions. Your staff must recognize that in some instances where you decide not to determine a measure for performance, this is not the result of a technical or strategic shortcoming, but is rather because you are convinced that the best way to assess this is based on a situational-driven analysis according to the prevailing circumstances. The ability to exercise judgement must take the highest ground, superseding any mathematical or mechanical systems. Detection of any risk-averse behaviour that is not in line with your strategy should be corrected immediately. Your 'bulls**t-detecting' capability should be enhanced, and it should be made highly visible. You should never let metrics or systems in place become constraints.

Next time you find yourself struggling with alignment questions, and with dilemmas about being lax versus being disciplined, ask yourself the following questions:

- Examine the areas in your organization where you think people are being lax: why are they being lax? Are the rules governing these areas still relevant? If yes then what is stopping you from enforcing them?
- Think of the time when an area started to become lax: what triggered it? What accelerated its development? Was this lax behaviour encouraged by your actions because it was an 'easy fix'? Did these actions eventually lead to more discipline? Did they solve the problem you initially faced?
- In a crisis, do you continue to promote orderliness? Do you continue to enforce your policies and procedures? If not, then why not? And if not, are people becoming more or less tempted to break rules continually? What will be the effect on your organization if breaking the rules becomes the norm?
- Reflect on how you react in an organizational confrontation: when you budge to pressure, what do you think you are signalling? Do you think people are more or less tempted to pressurize you now?
- Do you have a problematic area that you are 'accommodating' in your organization? Is the problem dissipating or being delayed? What other effects is it having on you and your organization? How do you think the presence of bad staff affects your good staff? Who do you think affects the other more? What is keeping you from getting rid of your bad staff and solving other problematic areas? What signals do you think you are giving out, when you stall in resolving these problems?

- What are your people's remuneration elements linked to? Are they aligned to your overall strategic goals?
- Do you have KPIs in place? Are they linked directly to fulfilling your strategic objectives? How flexible are they to accommodating any major context changes? Are they really helping your staff achieve what matters most? Does substance preside over form, when it comes to assessing the meeting of targets?

Epilogue: Post-crisis

Fast-forward to late 2017 and I'm in my London flat with three Syrian friends, watching live a highly anticipated Syrian encounter, at a time when a turning point was unfolding in the Syrian war. The war for Raqqa, the self-declared capital of ISIS, was nearing the end, with ISIS destined for a heavy defeat. Serious battles were also taking place near the city of Deir ez-Zor to break a siege that ISIS had imposed for a couple of years now. That highly anticipated encounter, amidst all these intense events, was happening in Tehran. It was a football game.

The Syrian national team had always been an average, or below-average, football team. We never made it to the World Cup. When we did end up qualifying for the regional Asian cup tournament, we never made it past the first round.

Between 2016 and 2017 something miraculous happened. In spite of the gruelling escalating war and the immense logistical and financial complications it caused, not to mention the obvious shifting of priorities, the Syrian national team played its best football ever and was as close as it ever came to making it to the World Cup.

FIFA had disallowed Syria from playing its home games in Syria. No neighbouring country agreed to host the Syrian team, to play its final round of home games. Thankfully, one nation in Asia eventually agreed, and that was Malaysia. Syria was to play its 'home' games in the final round 7,500 kilometres away from home. The Syrian football team was displaced and uprooted to a new 'home'. It was a logistical nightmare to round up the team at home anyway; the players now needed to meet in Damascus, coming from different Syrian cities and from abroad. They would then travel by bus to Beirut, where they would catch a plane to

Malaysia via a stopover in the Gulf. I doubt any sports team has ever had to travel for more than twenty-four hours to play at home. Add to that the effect of financial constraints, meaning that the Syrian team was allegedly unable to afford certain sportswear and some of the players chipped in themselves. The Syrian football coach earned around £300 a month. Hardly any other nation wanted to play a friendly game with Syria, for the team was viewed as 'rogue', an ugly duckling that no one wanted to be friends with – a total outcast.

In spite of all this, football miracles happened. The team slowly cruised past far more formidable opponents. We had to play the Chinese national team in China, which had invested millions of dollars in its football league in the past few years, attracting footballing superstars and paying them millions of dollars. Any of their fourteen-year-old Chinese 'water boys' on that match day probably earned more than the Syrian coach did. Marcello Lippi, later appointed China's coach, is reported to have had an annual salary of millions of pounds sterling. The different scale of the two teams was incomparable. It made sense, no matter how you viewed it, for China to win. But they didn't. Syria scored a beautiful solitary goal, which silenced thousands of Chinese fans in the stadium, and won that night. Many Syrians broadcast videos of Chinese people allegedly protesting in huge numbers outside the Chinese Football Association. Imagine the insult felt by many people in China – the most populous country in the world, which has invested hundreds of millions of pounds to improve its football, losing at home to the most war-battered country in the world. The Syrian team was on a winning streak and seemed almost invincible, invoking fear in their opponents as they marched sturdily towards the top positions of the group.

Their last game of the group, which my friends and I met to watch, was against Iran in Tehran. In past years the Iranian team has been one of Asia's best teams. In the qualifiers so far, they had earned the most points amongst all the teams. They had yet to concede a goal. No other team had scored even one goal against Iran in the final round of nine matches so far. If Syria were to win this game, they would make it for the first time ever to the World Cup. If they were to draw – provided a certain result stood in the other game, taking place between South Korea and Uzbekistan – they would make it to a new round of qualifying play-offs.

Thirteen minutes into the game, Syria scored! Iran had finally conceded a goal. Towards the end of the first half, Iran equalized. Twenty minutes into the second half, Iran scored a second goal. The Iranians were not going to slack, even if they had guaranteed qualification. My friends and I sat in the living room in despair, watching the dying minutes of the game as we started to accustom ourselves to the end of this fairy tale. We had enjoyed this fabulous journey and it was coming to a conclusion – or was it? Three minutes into injury time, the Syrian team intercepts the ball at midfield. Mardikian paces forward, finds Al Somah to his right and passes the ball to him. Al Somah receives the ball, composes himself, takes a look at the goal, finds an alluring gap and shoots it firmly between the goalkeeper's legs and . . . scores! My friends and I become hysterical – a euphoric moment when we erupt in joy and disbelief! This is by far the most ecstatic single moment I have ever felt. We jump up and down. We hug each other and scream in celebration. The unthinkable has happened. We have triumphed and are going to make it to the qualifying play-offs.

The Syrian commentator then broke down and cried. It was a triumph that transcended what you would typically feel for your team upon qualifying in the dying minutes, as there was another element to it. It wasn't merely a celebration of footballing skills. This was also a celebration of perseverance, resilience and showing your best at the worst of times. These are universally revered qualities that hardly anyone can fail to respect. How on earth could the Syrian team – a below-average side in competition, since the late 1940s – play its best football ever at the pinnacle of its epically devastating civil war? On paper, it did not make sense at all.

I would attribute a large part of this success to the resilience built up during the Syrian war. I strongly believe there are positives to be gained from any experience, and one should not allow the negatives – no matter how horrendously dominant they are – to prevent you from identifying the positives. If you were to ask the average outsider what they thought the Syrian team's aim should have been at the outset of the qualifiers, you would probably hear the response: either deciding not to take part or merely 'surviving' the qualifiers, because it did not make sense to compete seriously in such appalling circumstances. But that average outsider might not be aware of the positive outcomes of resilience. The Syrian football team later narrowly lost to Australia in their final leg in Sydney and just missed out on qualification. They had a free kick in the dying minutes and the ball struck the post. If only it had gone in . . . I still have dreams about that free kick.

Writing these lines in the comfort of my London home, a couple of years after my time in Syria and as I finalize this book, I reflect once again on the crisis I had to go through, which was experienced at all possible levels. Throughout this book my scope has been on building resilience in the workplace, not only to be able to withstand a crisis, but also to steer through it successfully and triumph. Experiences change those who go through them, on both an individual and an organizational level. It becomes harder to draw conclusions about how individuals change following a crisis, and this lies outside my expertise, as there are intricate psychological factors at play that seemingly do not apply to organizations. The argument becomes more complicated because an organization could be viewed as a composite of individuals who can transpose their own feelings onto that organization's actions and reactions. This could therefore create a philosophical debate on the extent to which certain traits that are normally applied to individuals can be applied to organizations or even to football teams, and the other way round.

I find that resilience yields three main positives, and this is based on my experience in a crisis, felt at all levels and stemming from my own involvement in the bank, along with first-hand exposure on the ground to the events in Syria, a nation over-whelmed by an epic crisis and one of the world's worst wars in contemporary times, which affected every household and every area of life – even its football team. The three positive traits that emerge are:

1. A chronic sense of indestructability
2. Vigorous self-awareness
3. A heightened *joie de vivre*.

I will address each of these positives below.

1 *A chronic sense of indestructability*

It took me the experience of the Syrian war to believe finally in the old adage 'what doesn't kill you makes you stronger'. What didn't kill the Syrian football team made them perform their best in the worst of times. With increasing resilience, you gradually start to gain a growing sense of fearlessness and near invincibility. A feeling that nothing can now destroy you emerges and may start to take a long-lasting form. Your former less-resilient self would have asked for survival at the outset of a crisis. Now you know better. You stop concerning yourself with mere 'survival' – who wants to survive, when they can actually grow and soar? This is why I have hardly used the word 'survival' in this book, unless I refer to it in a negative sense, which might come to a surprise for a book that revolves around war, crisis and resilience. The word 'survival' seems to be ever-present whenever crisis management is discussed. People typically love toying with this word, and using it extensively whenever a major complication arises.

The notion of survival really boils down to 'not dying'. That is not a state you should aspire to, in any circumstances. Your goal cannot be 'not dying'. It is only natural that you do not wish to die. You are probably feeling blessed for living and wish to prolong your life as much as possible, but that does not become a goal in itself. You have other goals to achieve, assuming that you are surviving. If the same applied to our bank and the Syrian football team in war, then it could apply to organizations working in far less-troubled crises. Even in war, our goal at the bank was to maximize the return for our shareholders. This happens by prospering and beating the competition. 'Not dying' will never maximize your return for shareholders.

Thinking along these lines proved vital to our mindset, and was something that dawned on us at the bank, without us consciously thinking about it. It would be difficult to apply many of the principles prescribed in this book if you are fixated on the notion of survival. The word 'survival' is used in the discipline of animal science, when talking about 'survival of the fittest'. Most animals' purpose in life is to live, eat and reproduce, so the word 'survival' befits them. I don't think it is productive to use this word in business.

At the outset of the Syrian war, many competing banks made the mistake of claiming that their outright objective was 'survival'. Whereas the term superficially invokes a quest for longevity and durability, most of the times the companies' actions resembled suicidal acts rather than acts of survival. When you are in distress, you should never give up your core elements in the hope of surviving. Many banks stopped lending and taking in deposits, because of the 'increasing inherent risk'. Just as supermarkets sell groceries, and restaurants serve food, banks are supposed to lend and take deposits. If a supermarket stops selling groceries, because of increasing risk, and claims it is doing so in order to survive, then it has actually taken the first step to end its own life. The banks in Syria that stopped lending completely reduced their risk-taking, for sure. The same ones that clamped down on their operations and restricted many of their services also enjoyed lower risks, as their actions stemmed from wanting to survive. However, time proved that these actions ultimately eroded the competitive capabilities of these banks. At BBSF we did not find solace in wanting to 'not die'. We knew there was a higher risk involved in continuing to manage in increasingly adverse times and we adapted accordingly, with the mindset of wanting to beat competition and reinforce ourselves as the number-one bank in Syria. If we were able to find opportunities in one of modern history's worst wars, then you are very likely to find similar opportunities in adverse circumstances.

If it weren't for the war, my life in Syria was so predictable that I could see how my whole life would unfold in front of me. I knew where I was going to live, who my friends were and what achievements I could realistically aspire to. I knew that I would always have a good job in banking, but I was never inclined to go beyond my comfort zone. Now, I find myself a changed person. The experience of crisis helped me never to fixate on mere survival, but always to think of growing, no matter what. This almost chronic sense of indestructability, which I hope will always stay with me, is something very valuable that I cherish, and which I would probably never have developed, had it not been for the crisis I went through.

2 Vigorous self-awareness

I studied for a minor degree in political sciences and was lucky to have a very talented political-sciences professor. I recall that, in one of his classes, he asked us to think about what forms a nation. We discussed the topic. The class offered many answers, such as a common language, religion, and so on. He then gave us two definitions for a nation – a cheeky one and a more serious one.

The cheeky one, by William Ralph Inge, Dean of St Paul's Cathedral, stated: 'A nation is a society united by a delusion about its ancestry and by a common hatred of its neighbours.' The second definition was that a nation is a group of people with a strong sense of collective history and a collective destiny.

Over the years I toyed with these ideas, as I extrapolated them to my own nation. Syria has many neighbours and, except for Israel, which annexed part of our land, Syrians generally did not dislike any of their other neighbours. Many Lebanese, however, were never fond of Syria, and I believe their perceived accentuated distinctiveness from Syria constitutes an essential part of their national psyche. But honestly, before the war, the feeling wasn't reciprocal. There was never really a general dislike of the Lebanese, Jordanians, Turks or Palestinians. As for our ancestry and collective feeling of a shared history, then one should note that the most prominent Arab nationalist schools of thought emerged from Syria. Pan-Arab nationalist ideologies that strive to unite twenty-two Arab countries had become so overpowering that they exceeded the more immediate sense of belonging to Syria, a land with its own incredibly unique, rich history. In Syrian Baathist doctrines, Syria is seen as being a temporary entity within its current borders, in the first phase of a much grander scheme that aspires to unite all Arab countries within one Arab nation. Before the war, when I renewed my passport in Damascus, it felt unnatural even to utter the word 'Syria' in public offices, when I needed to make references to leaving the country or entering it. The proper word was 'Al Qotor', which roughly translates as 'the small territory' – a Baathist term that refers to all Arab countries as territories that share a much loftier sense of belonging to the Arab nation.

A whole book can be written on Syrian national identity, but this does not lie within my scope. What concerns me is how the crisis changed things. Narrated stories about the Palmyrene Queen Zenobia fighting the Romans 1,800 years ago did not do much to create a collective history for Syrians. The same with drawing the bust on our banknotes of Philip the Arab, the Syrian emperor who ruled the Roman Empire in the third century AD. Even the legacy of the Umayyads – the first Arab empire that ruled a major part of the world from Damascus 1,400 years ago, and which is mentioned in the Syrian national anthem and is one of the most recognizable parts of our heritage – could not quite help forge that strong national identity. These memories were not relatable, and did not form an active and engaging sense of shared history. They could not be expected to unite someone from the Syrian desert, who looked, dressed and ate more like an Iraqi, with a fisherman from a Syrian Mediterranean town, who looked, dressed and ate more like a Greek.

It took a war to start reconceiving a rejuvenated national identity. We started to develop a collectively shared experience, even though it entailed many Syrians killing each other in the process. In the macro aspect of things, the Syrians from the desert and the Mediterranean can now relate to the tragedy that happened, even if at some stage of the war their families were at each other's throats. The Syrian tragedy, and the exodus that took place, instilled that sense of collective history. We now share an immediately relatable and tangible historical episode that we all experienced. And we have now come to be wary of our neighbours, in return. We saw at first hand how many Arab countries banned Syrians from visiting, even before the 'Trump ban'. I couldn't visit my parents in Kuwait for some time, even though I was born there and lived there for fourteen years; and I couldn't attend my best friend's wedding in Jordan. As I write these lines, I could not visit Egypt or Morocco on the occasions when I needed to. But I was able to travel to the US, and I continue to travel across Europe today. Since independence, governments in Syria have held out the pan-Arab banner, and all Arabs were able to visit Syria without requiring a visa, although this treatment was not reciprocal in most instances. But then many of the first countries to keep Syrians out were Arab, and one of the earliest discriminations that Syrians faced were in these Arab countries.

In the Lebanese suburb of Bourj Hammoud, just a few kilometres from Beirut, billboard banners were raised, clearly indicating a municipality-enforced curfew for Syrians, who were not to be on the street between evening and the early morning

hours. I don't think such discriminatory signs exist so casually anywhere else in the world. Most inhabitants of this suburb are
Lebanese of Armenian origin, whose ancestors had fled from Ana-
tolia into the wild Syrian desert around a hundred years ago,
following their mass-extermination in the last days of the Ottoman
Empire. Many of them were saved by the forefathers of the same
Syrian Arab tribes that had sent BBSF adulatory poems. My own
great-grandmother is Armenian, and was found by those tribes as
an orphan and rescued from the scorching desert. She was adopted
by a Damascene family and given a new identity, a new first name
and family name. Now imagine the bitterness Syrians felt, looking
at these banners prohibiting them from being on the streets, based
solely on where they came from – in a Lebanese town fewer than
sixty kilometres from the Syrian border, inhabited by an Armenian
majority. This would never happen in a German or Swedish town.
Most Syrians felt a collective sense of abandonment that they had
to yield to the perils of the sea up north, because the doors were
mostly shut towards their Arab 'brethren' in the south.

During the years preceding the war the overriding sentiment in
Syria was orientated to eclipse our sense of belonging to Syria in
favour of the greater Arab world, and to side with all its causes, but
it had now mostly abandoned us. That felt very bitter and hurtful.
Germany and Sweden, on the other hand – far-away neighbours
who have nothing to do with us – were surprisingly welcoming.
Such countries didn't differentiate between Syrians depending on
their political opinion, because they were viewed as Syrians from
the war who needed help, and this was what mattered to them. In
the long term I think this will create an almost unanimous feeling
among most Syrians, regardless of their sense of political belonging, that they ultimately have only each other and their shared land
in Syria.

I am certain that the crisis will in future give Syrians a stronger
collective sense of national identity. The tough times that Syrians
went through helped to forge a much stronger self-awareness, far
more effectively than all the other campaigns and attempts to

enforce a Syrian identity. It happened organically and naturally, and the evolving crisis fortified it. It is a spirited process that has still not ended, and which – in spite of the killings between Syrians today – I think will lead to a more cohesive Syria in the future.

A crisis stretches you, and enables you to explore your identify and test your abilities in a way that orderliness does not. You discover new things about yourself that you might not otherwise have known about. This builds a vigorous self-awareness that would have been very difficult to attain in orderly times. An organization emerging from a crisis can reflect on, and learn more about itself after a crisis. It will be in a much better position to determine its niche and its positioning, and how committed it really is towards its vision and mission. Has its vision evolved since before the crisis? If yes, then that could be attributed to increased self-awareness. If not, then this will fortify its identity and self-awareness, because in spite of the difficulties that were faced, its vision passed the test of tough times.

On a personal level, I discovered new aspects of myself that I knew little about. I became far more aware of my own strengths and limitations, and more propelled to focus on my growing niche interest in many areas. I have always had a fascination with history and food, but I never even thought about turning this into anything concrete, back in my days in Syria. In London, one of the most competitive cities in the world, I experimented with this fascination and created a series of events in museums with a historical theme. This was my niche – an area that was probably too geeky for others to have a passion about. The events that I created would sell out within the first few hours. This series of events, which I have called the 'Civilizations Supperclub', was chosen as one of the top-ten food experiences in the world by Lonely Planet – the only such event in London. I found immense purpose and joy in working on something that I felt very passionate about. When you find yourself in the uncomfortable realm of chaos and crisis, you emerge learning more about yourself, about what you want to do and what brings purpose to your life.

I would never in a million years have explored this side of me, if it wasn't for my growing sense of vigorous self-awareness.

3 *A heightened* joie de vivre

I have talked about the time a mortar bomb hit the same building I worked in, while I was there. What I did not disclose was that on that same day, later in the evening, my wife and I had dinner with friends in a restaurant in the same building. We laughingly joked during dinner that 'lightning never strikes the same place twice'. Crazy, right?

The last time I was in Damascus we were going out to a late-night party in the old city. As I sat in my grandmother's flat, with a western view of the horizon, waiting for my mother to dress up, I saw glaring lights and heard a big bomb. I called my wife, who was with her parents in another part of the city, and my sister-in-law picked up. 'You also heard that?' she said. I laughed and said yes. We turned on the news and, as expected, Israel had launched an air strike. My mother raced frantically into the living room and said she was not going out any more.

'Who in their right mind goes out during an air strike? People outside return home during an air strike. Not the other way round.'

'*Bil aks* – on the contrary,' I said. 'The best nights out are when *there are* air strikes.'

I spent more time in Syria during the war than my mother did, because relatively early on she travelled to Kuwait. I told her that several weeks from now she would look back on this night and cherish it as one of the best nights out ever in her life. I have no idea how I ultimately convinced her. We went out to the old city, to this beautifully renovated Damascene courtyard turned into a gastropub. As there were air strikes that night, the place became over-booked (yes, you read that correctly). The DJ started chanting anti-Israeli military lyrics, which excited the crowd, and the place went crazy. It was one of the best nights out ever. My mother still talks about it to this day.

We left the place in the old city, and I compared the street to how it was before the war. Before the war Damascus had a sleepy nightlife – a couple of bars concentrated in a few areas. It was nothing like the world-renowned nightlife of the neighbouring Lebanese capital, Beirut. Just as the nightlife in Beirut not only recovered, but became better during and after its fifteen-year civil war, so the same was happening in Damascus. Today, the nightlife in Damascus is the best it has ever been. Syrians – who are typically viewed as frugal and unpretentious, compared to their flashy, high-spending Lebanese neighbours – started to exhibit different traits. With war taking place, people began to appreciate the little pleasures of life more. Things that were taken for granted in the past were not taken for granted any longer. The tougher it became, the more people wanted to enjoy their time. A growing sense of *joie de vivre* emerged.

Mortar bombs would typically not hit Damascus in the early-morning hours or at night. As I spent most of my weekends in Beirut with my wife, the only time I really had to enjoy in Damascus was the early morning. A few friends at the bank who shared my love for food would meet up in the early hours before the military checkpoints got clogged up, and we would go and explore the many breakfast street-food chickpea eateries across the city. One chickpea place was so dirty that the server was holding a cigarette as he served us our *Fatteh*, the traditional poached-chickpea dish with tahini on a bed of croutons. He dropped some of his ash on to our dishes. We laughed so much, and we ate the whole plate. I still think it's the best *Fatteh* I have ever eaten.

In a crisis we learned to have a good time, no matter what, and to enjoy life. I stopped sweating the small stuff and became more focused on what is positive about what's going on.

Maybe this is the most important lesson that I personally took from the crisis. Resilience taught me to enjoy life's little pleasures, no matter what, even in the darkest of times. I also learned the concept of temporariness, which is surprisingly seldom mentioned as a noun, whereas the word 'permanence' is often used. I learned that virtually nothing in life is permanent. Almost everything is temporary. So why not try and have a good time at all times – even in the worst of times?

Whenever I feel down, I learned to recall the words of a medieval Sufi, who was once allegedly asked to write some words for a sultan that would instil an aura of optimism in him when he felt sad, and inject some rationality in him when he felt elated, because even in good times you should be mentally prepared for a change of circumstances.

His words were:

هذا الوقت سيمضي

This time shall pass.

Acknowledgements

There are two ways to do this: an awfully elaborate and emotional Syrian way or a half-page, brief and reserved British way. My heart says the former and my mind says the latter.

I will emphatically choose the former. I also fully realize that by limiting my options to two I just committed the false dichotomy logical fallacy that I addressed earlier – but since my heart is guiding this section I will let it pass.

I have a sister called Dana who is two years older than me but who really is my baby sister. She was born with complex learning and motor-skill disabilities and has special needs. Nothing pains me more than seeing her sad, not even after developing that sense of indestructability that I talked about earlier. She turned forty last summer yet thinks and acts like a nine-year-old girl who never grows older – she is like an eternal child. We call her at our home our *barakeh* – a blessing from God and our guardian angel. Her favourite thing in the world is ice cream and ever since I was young I would hold her hands and take her to the neighbourhood ice cream parlour every few days. I still do that to this day and nothing excites her more.

When I was fourteen I took her one day in Kuwait to the usual ice cream parlour and the old ice cream server welcomed us joyously as he always did. He asked me how I was doing. I told him I was happy as I had just changed schools – my parents had transferred me to the American school from the British school considering that I was destined to go to an American university rather than to a British one. I told him I was happier as the American school was much more lax: studies were far easier, we could choose the subjects we wanted, the dress code was very relaxed and we had so much more free time.

As the ice cream server scooped pistachio ice cream onto Dana's cup, he flinched and I saw a side of him that I hadn't seen before. Dana was eyeing the ice cream and cared less about what we were saying.

'You should be happiest when you are surrounded with those who challenge you and motivate you to achieve your best and not when you're with those who are lax with you.

'If I had people who challenged me growing up, I wouldn't be a sixty-year-old employed to sell ice cream.'

He jolted out these words before scooping Dana another generous serving of ice cream. I became a different person ever since.

I am blessed to have had many people who have constantly challenged me, motivated me and helped me grow to become the person that I am. Without them in my life, this book would never have seen the light of day.

It all starts with my amazing parents whom I am forever grateful for: my mother Salma and my father Ousama. My mother is a fountain of love who dedicated her life to her family and never stopped short of ensuring that she did the best she could for us. I remember in 1996 we moved from Kuwait to Dubai mid-year and no school would let me in at such an unusual time except for a very mediocre one where I started classes. But my mum did not stop searching for a much better school. She went around from one to another meeting the school principals and did not take no for an answer. She convinced the headmaster of a very good school to give me an exceptional entrance exam. I passed it and I joined this much better school the following week. I thank her for never settling for anything but the best for our family.

My school complications started earlier, actually. When the war broke out in Kuwait in 1990, I had no choice but to get enrolled in school in Damascus. My parents faced some liquidity difficulties as all of their savings were in Kuwaiti banks and this money suddenly became inaccessible. Luckily, my late uncle Hani Al Roumani, a renowned actor and director, was producing a historical soap opera revolving around events that took place around nine hundred years ago in Al-Andalus: what the Arabs called the Spanish region of Andalusia. He had a vacant position for an Arab knight that led armies. My father took this role. He had never ridden a horse in his life – now he had to pretend to be able to conquer all of Andalusia.

Large battle scenes were to be filmed near the Lebanese borders and plenty of horses were needed. The horses brought from the police academy were not enough so my uncle had no choice but to recruit horses that smugglers used near the borders. Both police and smuggler horses knew each other well in real life and now had to channel their real-life animosity to enact a historical battle. My father was given a fine smuggler's horse that befitted his role as a military commander – apparently the smugglers' horses were much fitter and much more resilient than the police's. Not a surprise since they operate in crisis and work for private enterprise.

The battles proved to be a little too intense for my father and the horse – in one of the battle scenes his horse heard the sound of sword clashes too closely and probably mistook it for the sound of border patrol bullets that he was used to. He became wild and ran frantically. Wearing heavy tenth-century Arab military armour and a helmet while holding a sword made the task of controlling the horse even more colossal – my father fell and broke his arm and bruised his entire body. It became increasingly difficult continuing the role – but he did. His Arab knight character continued beating armies. I later learned that on the day he received his pay for the role, he paid almost all of it towards my tuition fees in one of Damascus' very few international schools. He would do anything for me – even if it meant conquering half of Spain with a broken arm and on a short-tempered horse. He is my role model in life.

Then there's my wife and the love of my life: Nadeen. If there is one thing harder than tolerating your partner working in a war-zone with the constant threat of mortar bombs, it probably is tolerating your partner's 'writing'. I think there is a special place in heaven for the partners of first-time aspirational writers and there will be an even more special spot for Nadeen, who never lost faith in me and in my writing. From tolerating my days sitting at home and writing, to handling my swinging writer moods, to rereading the early drafts and to never stopping short of consistently giving me valuable feedback. This book would never have seen the light if it weren't for her constant support and love.

Big gratitude to my most amazing in-laws Prof. Zohair Haidar and Faten Lahham. They paved the way for our move to London and were of immense support. No one could have ever wished for more loving in-laws.

There's Zeina, my beautiful and inspirational younger sister – I can't stop staring at the photos of her beautiful baby Reina throughout my days. I thank her for always standing with me and for tolerating her elder and sometimes annoying brother.

I thank my Grandfather Fares Eid who passed away a few years ago. When I walk the streets of London I can't help but every few days remember the first time I came here with him as a child. He loved this city and lived here for a while as a Syrian military pilot being trained by the British Air Force in the early 1950s. He was a principled man who taught me a lot in life. I also thank my grandmother Afaf, who is one of the most loving and patient people ever. I learned a lot from her and love her so much.

Then there are those special ones who come along in your life and change it forever. I would be less of a person if it wasn't for my best friend Bisher Challah. Even if I had a brother, I don't think he would be as close to me as Bisher is. I thank him for being there in my life.

I am also blessed to have had and continue to have a mentor that one could only dream of: Mr Riad Obegi – the most intelligent person I have ever met. Every minute I spend with him is a minute that stimulates my intellect and makes me grow. If there is any shred of wisdom in this book, it probably is somehow influenced by him. If there is anything that is unworthy, then he must have had absolutely nothing to do with it.

Thanks also to the following who know very well the support they offered me in different ways. My uncle Maher Roumani and his wife Anna, who helped us greatly when we first moved to

London. Then there's Jihad Massoud, Ali Ammoura, Nader Ajami, Rami Saltagi, Taleb Ghazal, Anas Diab, Ibrahim Alturki, Iyad Elhallak, Oliver Zeitoun and his amazing family, Zahar Mejanni, Sami Ouzon and Mido Sahyouni.

Moving on to the UK, I wish to thank my literary agent Ben Clark from the Soho Agency for believing in this work and taking it forward. I am lucky to have him represent me. I remember the time he told me we had a meeting at Penguin who were interested in my book. As a boy in Damascus and Kuwait I grew up devouring Roald Dahl's books with the iconic Quentin Blake illustrations and the Penguin imprint. I always dreamt of writing a book some day. Walking to the meeting room at Penguin headquarters at the Strand in London was one of the most exciting moments in my life. In that meeting I met Martina O'Sullivan, the Editorial Director of Penguin Business. I was blown away by her passionate thoughts on my book and I knew my book would find a beautiful home at Penguin. Thanks to Martina's valuable comments and feedback, I spent the next few months working mostly on my weekends on improving the book's structure and scope. She made working on weekends one of my most pleasurable moments of the week – that's how good she was. I also thank the rest of the fabulous team at Penguin Random House: Celia Buzuk, Natalie Wall, and the others. Then there's Mandy Greenfield the copy-editor, and Justine Stoddart the photographer. I also thank the other reputable publishers and literary agents that showed interest in my book.

There is a group of friends that have taken the time in the very early draft versions of the book to go through it and share some feedback when some of the ideas were still fuzzy and the structure in disarray but they encouraged me to go on. I thank them all: Anas Halabi, Charlie Serocold, Hani Khatib, Karim Khwanda, Louay Wanli, Nabil Chaachou, Paulina Delgado Salazar, Pedro Calmell Del Solar and Saleh Rustom.

I also thank all my colleagues at BBSF across all levels that I have worked with since my first day there in February 2006 until June

2015 – the list is too long to write and I apologize for not being able to list them one by one. I learned so much from many of them.

I have been through two wars but I feel blessed – thanks be to God.

A final word on my fellow Syrian women and men. Probably no other people on earth in contemporary times have had to go through the hardships and misfortunes that Syrians have. It is the kind of belonging that can be troublesome and so inconvenient but at the same time one that is miraculously beautiful and warm. In spite of the difficulties that I had lived through in Syria even when mortar bombs rained over me, they are nothing compared to the much more tragic circumstances that most other Syrians went through.

My love goes out to all of them – and to my beloved Syria.

Louai Al Roumani
8 September, 2019
London

PENGUIN PARTNERSHIPS

Penguin Partnerships is the Creative Sales and Promotions team at Penguin Random House. We have a long history of working with clients on a wide variety of briefs, specializing in brand promotions, bespoke publishing and retail exclusives, plus corporate, entertainment and media partnerships.

We can respond quickly to briefs and specialize in repurposing books and content for sales promotions, for use as incentives and retail exclusives as well as creating content for new books in collaboration with our partners as part of branded book relationships.

Equally if you'd simply like to buy a bulk quantity of one of our existing books at a special discount, we can help with that too. Our books can make excellent corporate or employee gifts.

Special editions, including personalized covers, excerpts of existing books or books with corporate logos can be created in large quantities for special needs.

We can work within your budget to deliver whatever you want, however you want it.

For more information, please contact
salesenquiries@penguinrandomhouse.co.uk